BETTY GORDON AT MOUNTAIN CAMP

Or, The Mystery of Ida Bellethorne

ALICE B. EMERSON

1st WORLD
LIBRARY
Literary Society

Betty Gordon at Mountain Camp

Alice B. Emerson

© 1st World Library, 2007
PO Box 2211
Fairfield, IA 52556
www.1stworldlibrary.com
First Edition

LCCN: 2007934074

Softcover ISBN: 978-1-4218-9607-6
Hardcover ISBN: 978-1-4218-9707-3
eBook ISBN: 978-1-4218-9507-9

Purchase *"Betty Gordon at Mountain Camp"*
as a traditional bound book at:
www.1stWorldLibrary.com/purchase.asp?ISBN=978-1-4218-9607-6

1st World Library is a literary, educational organization
dedicated to:

- Creating a free internet library of downloadable ebooks

- Hosting writing competitions and offering book publishing
scholarships.

Interested in more 1st World Library books? contact:
literacy@1stworldlibrary.com
Check us out at: www.1stworldlibrary.com

1ˢᵗ World Library Literary Society

Giving Back to the World

"If you want to work on the core problem, it's early school literacy."

- James Barksdale, former CEO of Netscape

"No skill is more crucial to the future of a child, or to a democratic and prosperous society, than literacy."

- Los Angeles Times

"Literacy... means far more than learning how to read and write... The aim is to transmit... knowledge and promote social participation."

- UNESCO

"Literacy is not a luxury, it is a right and a responsibility. If our world is to meet the challenges of the twenty-first century we must harness the energy and creativity of all our citizens."

- President Bill Clinton

"Parents should be encouraged to read to their children, and teachers should be equipped with all available techniques for teaching literacy, so the varying needs and capacities of individual kids can be taken into account."

- Hugh Mackay

CONTENTS

I. THE ORANGE SILK OVER-BLOUSE 9

II. THE FRUITS OF TANTALUS 18

III. OFF FOR A GALLOP..25

IV. A SECOND IDA BELLETHORNE 30

V. MEASLES...42

VI. A DISAPPEARANCE..50

VII. ALL MRS. STAPLES COULD SAY 57

VIII. UNCLE DICK MUST BE TOLD..................................64

IX. THE LIVE WIRE OCTETTE..70

X. BEAUTIFUL SNOW..79

XI. STALLED, AND WITHOUT A DOCTOR 86

XII. THE TUNNEL 93

XIII. AN ALARM.. 100

XIV. THE MOUNTAIN HUT.. 106

XV. THE LOST GIRL.. 115

XVI. THE CAMP ON THE OVERLOOK 121

XVII. OFF ON SNOWSHOES.. 128

XVIII. GREAT EXCITEMENT 136

XIX. THE EMERGENCY 143

XX. BETTY'S RIDE.. 148

XXI. BETTY COMES THROUGH 154

XXII. ON THE BRINK OF DISCOVERY 161

XXIII. CAN IT BE DONE?.. 166

XXIV. TWENTY MILES OF GRADE.............................. 173

XXV. ON THE DECK OF THE SAN SALVADOR.......... 182

CHAPTER I

THE ORANGE SILK OVER-BLOUSE

"This doesn't look like the street I came up through!" exclaimed Betty Gordon. "These funny streets, with their dear old-fashioned houses, all seem, so much alike! And if there are any names stuck up at the corners they must hide around behind the post when I come by like squirrels in the woods.

"I declare, there is a queer little shop stuck right in there between two of those refined-looking, if poverty-stricken, boarding-houses. Dear me! how many come-down-in-the-world families have to take 'paying guests' to help out. Not like the Peabodys, but really needy people. What is it Bobby calls 'em? 'P.G.s'—'paying guests.'

"I was a paying guest at Bramble Farm," ruminated Betty, still staring at the little shop and the houses that flanked it on either side. "And I certainly had a hard time there. Bobby says that these people in Georgetown are the remains of Southern aristocracy that were cast up on this beach as long ago as the Civil War. Unlike the castaways on cannibal islands that we read about, Bobby says these castaways live off the 'P.G.s'—and that's what Joseph Peabody tried to do! He tried to live off me. There! I knew he was a cannibal.

"Oh! Isn't that sweet?"

Her sudden cry had no reference to the army of boarding-house keepers in the neighborhood, nor to any signpost that pointed the way back to the little square where the soldiers' monument stood and where Betty was to meet Carter, the Littells' chauffeur, and the big limousine. For she was still staring at the window of the little shop.

"What a lovely orange color! And that starburst pattern on the front! It's lovely! What a surprising thing to see in a little neighborhood store like this. I'm going to buy it if it fits me and I've money enough left in my purse."

Impetuous as usual, Betty Gordon marched at once to the door of the little side-street shop. The most famous of such neighborhood shops, as described by Hawthorne, Betty knew all about. She had studied it in her English readings at Shadyside only the previous term. But there was no Gingerbread Man in this shop window!

In the middle of the display window, which was divided into four not very large panes, was arranged on a cross of bright metal a knitted over-blouse of the very newest burnt orange shade. The work was exquisitely done, as Betty could see even from outside the shop, and she did hope it would fit her.

On pushing open the door a silvery bell—not an annoying, jangling bell—played a very lively tune to attract the attention of a girl who sat at the back of the shop, her head bent close above the work on which she was engaged. Although the bell stopped quivering when Betty closed the door, the girl did not look up from her work.

Sharp-eyed Betty saw that the stranger was knitting, and she seemed to be engaged upon another over-blouse like that in

Alice B. Emerson

the window, save that the silk in her lap was of a pretty dark blue shade. Betty saw her full, red lips move placidly. The girl was counting over her work and she actually was so deeply immersed in the knitting that she had not heard the bell or realized that a possible customer had entered.

"Ahem!" coughed Betty.

"And that's twenty-four, and—cross—and two—and four—" The girl was counting aloud.

"Why," murmured Betty Gordon, her eyes dancing, "she's like Libbie Littell when she is somnambulating—I guess that is the right word. Anyway, when Libbie walks in her sleep she talks just like that—

"*Ahem!*"

This time Betty almost shouted the announcement of her presence in the shop and finally startled the other girl out of her abstraction. The latter looked up, winked her eyes very fast, and began to roll up her work in a clean towel. Betty noticed that her eyes were very blue and were shaded by dark lashes.

"I beg your pardon," said the shopgirl. "Have you been waiting long?" She came forward quickly and with an air of assurance. Her look was not a happy one, however, and Betty wondered at her sadness. "What can I show you?" asked the shopgirl.

She was not much older than Betty herself, but she was more self-possessed and seemed much more experienced than even Betty, much as the latter had traveled and varied as her adventures had been during the previous year and a half. But now the stranger's questions brought Betty to a renewed comprehension of what she had actually entered the shop for.

"I'm just crazy about that blouse in the window—the orange one," she cried. "I know you must have made it yourself, for you are knitting another, I see, and that is going to be pretty, too. But I want this orange one—if it doesn't cost too much."

"The price is twelve dollars. I hope it is not too much," said the shopgirl timidly. "I sold one for all of that before I left Liverpool."

Betty was as much interested now in the other girl as she was in the orange silk over-blouse.

"Why!" she exclaimed, "you are English, aren't you? And you and your family can't long have been over here."

"I have been here only two months," said the girl quietly.

There was a certain dignity in her manner that impressed Betty. She had very dark, smoothly arranged hair and a beautiful complexion. She was plump and strongly made, and she walked gracefully. Betty had noted that fact when she came forward from the back of the shop.

"But you didn't come over from England all alone?" asked the curious young customer, neglecting the blouse for her interest in the girl who spread out its gossamer body for approval.

"It took only seven days from Liverpool to New York," said the other girl, looking at Betty steadily, still with that lack of animation in her face. "I might have come alone; but it was better for me to travel with somebody, owing to the emigration laws of your country. I traveled as nursemaid to a family of Americans. But I separated from them in New

Alice B. Emerson

York and came here."

"Oh!" Betty exclaimed, not meaning to be impertinent. "You had friends here in Georgetown?"

"I thought I had a relative in Washington. I had heard so. I failed to find her so—so I found this shop, kept by a woman who came from my county, and she gave me a chance to wait shop," said the English girl wearily.

"Mrs. Staples lets me knit these blouses to help out, for she cannot pay large wages. The trade isn't much, you see. This one, I am sure, will look lovely on you. I hope the price is not too much?"

"Not a bit, if it will fit me and I have that much money in my purse," replied Betty, who for a girl of her age had a good deal of money to spend quite as she pleased.

She opened her bag hastily and took out her purse. The purse was made of cut steel beads and, as Betty often said, "everything stuck to it!" Something clung to it now as she drew it forth, but neither Betty nor the shopgirl saw the dangling twist of tissue paper.

"And I'll buy that other one you are knitting," Betty hurried to say as she shook the purse and dug into it for the silver as well as the bills she had left after her morning's shopping. "I know that pretty blue will just look dear on a friend of mine."

She was busy with her money, and the English girl looked on hopefully. So neither saw the twist of tissue paper fly off the dangling fringe of beads and land with a soft little "plump" on the floor by the counter.

"Dear me!" breathed the shopgirl, in reply to Betty's promise,

"I shall like that. It will help a good bit—and everything so high in this country. A dollar, as you say, goes hardly anywhere! And this one will fit you beautifully. You can see yourself."

"Of course it will. Do it up at once," cried the excited Betty. "Here is the money. Twelve dollars. I was afraid I didn't have enough. And be sure and keep that blue one for my friend. Maybe she will come for it herself, so give me a card or something so she can find the place. Shall she ask for you?"

"If you please," and the English girl ran to write a card. She brought it back with the neatly made parcel of the over-blouse and slipped it into Betty Gordon's hand. The latter thanked her and looked swiftly at the name the other had written.

"Good-bye, Ida Bellethorne," she said, smiling. "What a fine name! I hope I can sell some more blouses for you. I'll try."

The shopgirl made a little bow and the silvery bell jangled again as Betty opened the door. Betty looked back at the English girl, and the latter looked after Betty. They were both interested, much interested, the one in the other, and for reasons that neither suspected. Ida Bellethorne was not much like the girls Betty knew. She seemed even more sedate than the seniors at Shadyside where Betty had attended school with the Littell girls since the term had opened in September.

Ida Bellethorne was not, however, in any such happy condition as the girls Betty Gordon knew. She might have told the warm-hearted customer who had bought the over-blouse a story that would indeed have spurred Betty's interest to an even greater degree. But the English girl was naturally of a secretive disposition, and she was among strangers.

Alice B. Emerson

She turned back into the store when Betty had gone and the door, swinging shut, set the bell above it jingling again. A door opened at the end of the room and a tall, aggressive woman in a long, straight, gingham frock strode into the room. She had very black, heavy brows that met over her nose and this, with the thick spectacles she wore, gave her a very stern expression.

"What's the matter with that bell, Ida?" she demanded, in a sharp voice. "It seems to ring enough, but it doesn't ring any money into my cash-drawer as I can see."

"I sold my over-blouse out of the window, Mrs. Staples," said the girl.

"Humph! What else?"

"Er—what else? Why—why, she said she might come back for the one I am making."

"Humph!" ejaculated Mrs. Staples a second time. "I don't see as that will fill my cellar with coal. Couldn't you sell her anything else out of the shop?"

"She didn't say she wanted anything else," said Ida timidly.

"Oh! She didn't? You'll never make a sales-woman till you learn to sell 'em things they don't want but that the shop wants to sell. And I was foolish enough to tell you that you could have all you could make out of those blouses. Oh, well! I'm always being foolishly generous. Come! What's that on the floor? Pick it up."

Mrs. Staples was very near-sighted, yet nothing seemed to escape her observation. She pointed to the twist of white tissue paper on the floor which had been twitched out of

Betty Gordon's bag. Ida stooped as she was commanded and got the paper. She was about to toss it into the waste-basket behind the counter when she realized that there was some hard object wrapped in the paper.

"What is it?" asked Mrs. Staples, in her quick, stern way, as she saw Ida open the twist of paper.

"Why, I—Oh, Mrs. Staples! look what this is, will you?"

She held out in the palm of her hand a little, heart-shaped platinum locket with a tiny but very beautiful diamond set in the center of its face, and when she turned it over on the back was engraved the intertwined letters "E.G."

"For the land's sake!" ejaculated Mrs. Staples, coming nearer and grabbing the locket out of Ida's hand. "Where did you get this?"

"Why, Mrs. Staples, you saw me pick it up."

"But how did it come there?"

"Oh, I know!" Ida Bellethorne cried, with sudden animation. "That girl stood right there. She opened her bag to get out her purse and she must have flirted it out to the floor."

"Humph!" said the storekeeper doubtfully.

"Give it to me, Mrs. Staples, and I'll run after her," cried the English girl anxiously.

"Humph!" This was Mrs. Staples' stock ejaculation and expressed a variety of emotions. Just now it expressed doubt. "And then you'd come back and tell me how thankful she was to get it, while maybe it doesn't belong to her at all. No,"

Alice B. Emerson

said Mrs. Staples, "let her come looking for it if she lost it."

"Oh!" murmured Ida Bellethorne doubtfully.

"Perhaps she will never guess she dropped it here."

"That's no skin off your nose," declared the vulgar shop-woman. "You've no rights in this thing, anyway. What's found on the floor of my shop is just as much mine as what's on the counter or in the trays behind the counter. I know my rights. Until whoever lost this thing comes in and proves property, it's mine."

"Oh, Mrs. Staples!" cried her employee. "Is that the law in this country? It doesn't seem honest."

"Humph! It's honest enough for me. And who are you, I'd like to know, a greenhorn fresh from the old country, trying to tell me what's honest and what ain't? If that girl comes back—"

"Yes, Mrs. Staples?"

"You sell her that other blouse if you want to, or anything else out of the shop. But you keep your mouth shut about this locket unless she asks for it. Understand? I won't have no tattle-tales about me; and if you don't learn when to keep your mouth open and when to keep it shut, I'll have no use at all for you in my shop. Remember that now!"

CHAPTER II

THE FRUITS OF TANTALUS

Betty Gordon had glanced hastily at her wrist watch as she went out of the little store. It was very near the minute appointed for her to meet Carter at the square. And she had forgotten to ask that girl, Ida Bellethorne (such an Englishy name!), how to find her rendezvous with the Littells' chauffeur.

She hesitated, tempted to run back. Had she done so she would have been in time to see Ida pick up the little locket that Uncle Dick had given Betty that very Christmas and which she carried in her bag because it seemed the safest place to treasure it while she was visiting. Her trunk was at Shadyside.

So it is that the very strangest threads of romance are woven in this world. And Betty Gordon had found before this that her life, at least, was patterned in a very wonderful way. Since she had been left an orphan and had found her only living relative, Mr. Richard Gordon, her father's brother, such a really delightful guardian the girl had been to so many places and her adventures had been so exciting that her head was sometimes quite in a whirl when she tried to think of all the happenings.

Uncle Dick's contracts with certain oil promotion companies made it impossible as yet for him to have what Betty thought of as "a real, sure-enough home." He traveled here, there and everywhere. Betty loved to travel too; but Uncle Dick was forced to go to such rough and wild places that at first he could not see how Betty, a twelve year old, gently bred girl, could go with him.

Therefore he had to find a home for his little ward for a few months, and remembering that an old school friend of his was married to the owner of a big and beautiful farm, he arranged for Betty to stay with the Peabodys at Bramble Farm. Her adventures as a "paying guest" in the Peabody household are fully related in the first book of the series, entitled "Betty Gordon at Bramble Farm," and a very exciting experience it was.

In spite, however, of the disagreeable and miserly Joseph Peabody, Betty would not have missed her adventures at the farm for anything. In the first place, she met Bob Henderson there, and a better boy-chum a girl never had than Bob. Although Bob had been born and brought up in a poorhouse, and at first knew very little about himself and his relatives, even a girl like Betty could see that this "poorhouse rat" as he was slurringly called by Joseph Peabody, possessed natural refinement and a very bright mind.

Betty and Bob became loyal friends, and when Betty, in the second volume, called "Betty Gordon in Washington," had fairly to run away from Bramble Farm to meet her Uncle Dick in the national capital, badly treated Bob ran away likewise, on the track of somebody who knew about his mother's relatives. Betty's adventures in Washington began with a most astonishing confusion of identities through which she met the Littells—a charming family consisting of a Mr. Littell, who was likewise an "Uncle Dick"; a motherly

Mrs. Littell, who never found young people—either boys or girls—troublesome; three delightful sisters named Louise, Roberta, and Esther Littell; and a Cousin Elizabeth Littell, who good-naturedly becomes "Libbie" instead of "Betty" so as not to conflict in anybody's mind with "Betty" Gordon.

The fun they all had in Washington while Betty waited for the appearance of her real Uncle Dick, especially after Bob Henderson turned up and was likewise adopted for the time being by the Littell family, is detailed to the full in that second story. And at last both Betty and Bob got news from Oklahoma, where Mr. Richard Gordon was engaged, which set them traveling westward in a great hurry—Betty to meet Uncle Dick at Flame City and her boy chum hard on the trace of two elusive aunts of his, his mother's sisters, who appeared to be the only relatives he had in the world.

Betty and Bob discovered the aunts just in time to save them from selling their valuable but unsuspected oil holdings to sharpers, and in "Betty Gordon in the Land of Oil" one of the most satisfactory results that Betty saw accomplished was the selling of the old farm for Bob and his aunts for ninety thousand dollars.

Uncle Dick decided that Betty must go to a good school in the fall, and they chose Shadyside because the Littells and their friends were going there. Bob, now on a satisfactory financial plane, arranged to attend the Salsette Military Academy which was right across the lake from the girls' boarding school, Uncle Dick, who was now Bob's guardian, having advised this.

Hastening back from Oklahoma, while Uncle Dick was called to Canada to examine a promising oil field there, Betty and Bob met the girls and boys they previously got acquainted with in Washington and some other friends, and

Alice B. Emerson

Betty at least began her boarding school experience with considerable confidence as well as delight.

It was not all plain sailing as subsequent events prove; yet in "Betty Gordon at Boarding School," the fourth volume of the series, Betty had many; pleasant adventures as well as school trials. She was particularly interested in the fortunes of Norma and Alice Guerin, who had been Betty's friends when she was living at Bramble Farm; and it was through Betty's good offices that great happiness came to the Guerin girls and their parents.

The hospitable Littells had invited their daughters' school friends (and, to quote Bob, there was a raft of them!) to come to Fairfields for the Christmas holidays, and at the close of the first term they bade good-bye to Shadyside and Salsette and took the train for Washington.

Fairfields, which was over the river in Virginia, was one of the most delightful homes Betty Gordon had ever seen. It was closer to Georgetown than to the nation's capital, and that is why Betty on this brisk morning was shopping in the old-fashioned town and had come across the orange silk over-blouse in the window of the neighborhood shop.

It was really too bad that Betty did not run back to the shop to ask for directions to the soldiers' monument square. She would have been just in season to interrupt the scene between Ida Bellethorne and Mrs. Staples and before the latter had threatened Ida with dismissal if she told Betty about the tiny locket. When she came to find it out, this loss of Uncle Dick's present, was going to trouble Betty Gordon very much.

"Where in the world can that soldiers' monument be?" murmured Betty to herself as, after hurrying on for a distance and having turned two corners, she found herself in a neighborhood that looked stranger than ever to her.

Not a soul was in sight at that moment, but presently she saw a small negro boy shuffling along, drawing a piece of chalk on the various houses and stoops as he passed.

"Boy, come here!" called Betty to the little fellow.

At once the colored boy stopped the use of his piece of chalk and stared at her with wide-open eyes.

"I ain't done nuffin, lady, 'deed I ain't," he mumbled, and then began to back away.

"I only want to know where the soldiers' monument is," she returned. "Do you know?"

"Soldiers' monument am over that way," and the boy waved his hand to one side, where there was a hilly street, and then hurried out of sight.

"Oh, dear! that's not very definite," sighed Betty.

But now she ran down the hilly street at a chance, turned a crooked corner and came plump upon the square and the soldiers' monument. There was the Littells' big, closed car just turning into the square from another street.

"What luck! Fancy!" gasped Betty, running swiftly to the place where the big car stopped.

"You're better than prompt, Miss Betty," said the driver of the car. "I am glad I hadn't to wait for you, for Mister Bob told me particular to get you home for luncheon. You'll be wanted."

Alice B. Emerson

"What for? Do tell me what for, Carter!" Betty cried. "I thought Bob Henderson was awfully mysterious this morning at breakfast. Do you know what is in the wind, Carter?"

"Not me, Miss Betty," said the chauffeur, and having tucked the robes about her he shut the door and got into his own place. But before he started the car he said through the open window: "I have to delay a little, Miss. Must drive around by the bank and pick up Mr. Gordon. But I will hurry home after that."

"Oh! Uncle Dick did go to the bank here," murmured Betty, nestling back into the cushions and robes. "I wonder if he is going to stop off at Mountain Camp on his way back to Canada. Oh!" and she sighed more deeply, "if we could only go up there with him—"

The car stopped before the gray stone bank building. Uncle Dick seemed to have been on the watch for them, he came out so promptly. Although his hair was graying, especially about the temples, Mr. Richard Gordon was by no means an old looking man. He lived much out of doors and spent such physical energy only as his out-of-door life yielded, instead of living on his reserve strength as so many office-confined men do. Betty had learned all about that in physics. She was thoroughly an out-of-door girl herself!

"Oh, Uncle Dick!" she cried when he stepped into the car, "are you really and truly getting ready to go north again?"

"Must, my dear. Have still some work to do in spite of the ice and snow in Canada. And, as I told you, I mean to stop and see Jonathan Canary."

"That is what I mean, Uncle Dick," she cried. "Will you go

to that lovely Mountain Camp all alo-o-one?"

"Mercy me, child, you never saw it—and in winter! You do not know whether it is lovely or not."

"It must be," said Betty warmly, "You have explained it all so beautifully to us. The lovely lake surrounded by hills, and the long toboggan slide, and the skating, and fishing for pickerel through the ice, and—Oh, dear me! if we can't go—"

"If who can't go?" demanded her uncle in considerable amazement.

"Why, me. And Bob. And Bobby Littell and Louise, and the Tucker twins, and all the rest. We were talking about it last night. It—would—be—won—der—ful!"

"Well, of all the—Why, Betty!" exclaimed Mr. Gordon, "you know you must go right back to school."

"Yes, I know," sighed Betty. "It is like the fruits of Tantalus, isn't it? We read about him in Greek mythology—poor fellow! He stood up to his chin in water and over his head hung the loveliest fruits. But when he stooped to get a drink the water receded, and when he stood on tiptoe to reach the fruit, they receded too. It was dreadful! And Mountain Camp, where your friend Mr. Canary lives, is just like that. Uncle Dick. For us it is the fruits of Tantalus."

Uncle Dick stared at her for a moment, then he burst out laughing. But Betty Gordon remained perfectly serious until they arrived at Fairfields.

Alice B. Emerson

CHAPTER III

OFF FOR A GALLOP

The crowd at the Littell lunch table (and it was literally a "crowd" although the Guerin girls and some of the other over Christmas visitors had already gone home) hailed Betty's arrival vociferously.

"How do you stand it?" asked Uncle Dick, smiling at Mrs. Littell who presided at one end of the table. "I should think they would drive you distracted."

Mrs. Littell laughed jovially and beamed at her young company. "I am only distracted when Mr. Littell and I are here alone," she rejoined. "This is what keeps us young."

"You've only a shake to eat in, Betty," exclaimed Bobby Littell, who was very dark and very gay and very much alive all of the time. "Do hurry. We're 'most through."

"Dear me! what can I eat in a shake?" murmured Betty, as the soup was placed before her. "And I am hungry."

"A milk-shake should be absorbed in a shake," observed Bob Henderson, grinning at her from across the table.

"I need more than that, Bob, after what I have been through this morning. Such a job as shopping is! And oh, Bobby! I've got the loveliest thing to show you. You'll just squeal!"

"What is it?" cried Bobby, eager and big-eyed at once. "Do hurry your luncheon, Betty. We've all got to change, and it's almost time."

"Time for what?" demanded Betty, trying to eat daintily but hurriedly.

But Mrs. Littell called them to order here. "Give Betty time to eat properly. Whatever it is, Betty, it can't begin until you are ready."

"I'm through, Mother," said Bobby. "May I be excused? I'll have to help Esther, you know. You'd better forget your appetite, Betty," she whispered as she passed the latter on her way out of the room. "Time and tide wait for no man—or girl either."

"What does she mean?" wondered Betty, and became a little anxious as the others began to rise, too, and were excused. "Have we got to change? What is it—the movies? Or a party? Of course, it isn't skating? Even if there was a little scale of ice last night, it would never in this world bear us," added Betty, utterly puzzled.

Bob Henderson had slipped around to her side of the table and leaned over her chair back to whisper in Betty's ear:

"You've got to be ready in twenty minutes. The horses won't stand this cold weather—not under saddle."

"Saddle! Horses!" gasped Betty Gordon, rising right up from the table with the soup spoon in her hand. "I—I don't believe

I want any more luncheon, Mrs. Littell. Really, I don't need any more. Will you please excuse me?"

"Not if you run away with my spoon, Betty," laughed her hostess. "It was the dish that ran away with the spoon, and you are not a dish, dear."

"She'll be dished if she doesn't hurry," called Bob from the door, and then he disappeared.

"Sit down and finish your luncheon, Betty," advised Mrs. Littell. "I assure you that they will not go without you. The men can walk the horses about a little if it is necessary."

"I haven't been in a saddle since I left the land of oil and my own dear Clover-pony!" cried Betty later, as she ran upstairs. "I know just where my riding habit is. Oh, dear! I hope I have as spirited a horse as dear Clover was. Are you all ready, Bobby? And you, too, Louise—and Esther? Goodness me! suppose Carter had broken down on the road and hadn't brought me back in time—

"Libbie! For goodness' sake don't sit down in that chair. That package has got the loveliest orange silk over-blouse in it. Wait till you see it, Bobby."

She fairly dragged the plump girl, Libbie, away from the proximity of the chair in question and then began to scramble into her riding dress. The clatter of hoofs was audible on the drive as she fixed the plain gold pin in her smart stock.

"Of course," Betty said with a sigh, "one can't wear a locket, with or without a chain, when one is riding. That dear locket Uncle Dick gave me! I suppose it is safe enough in my bag. Well, I'm ready."

They all ran down to the veranda to see the mounts. Betty's was a beautiful gray horse named Jim that she had seen before in the Fairfields stables.

"He's sort of hard-bitted, Miss," said the smiling negro who held the bridle and that of Bobby's own pony, a beautiful bay. "But he ain't got a bad trick and is as kind as a lamb, Miss."

"Oh, I'm not afraid of him," declared Betty. "You ought to see my Clover. All right, Uncle Dick, I'm up!"

They were all mounted and cantering down the drive in a very few minutes. Even plump little Libbie sat her steed well, for she had often ridden over her own Vermont hills.

"I don't know where we're going, but I'm on my way!" cried Betty, who was delighted to be once more in the saddle.

"We're going right across country to Bolter's stock farm," Louise told her. "Here's where we turn off. There will be some fences. Can you jump a fence, Betty?"

"I can go anywhere this gray horse goes," declared Betty proudly.

But Bob rode up beside her before they came to the first jump. "Look out for the icy places, Betsey," he warned her. "None of these horses are sharpened. They never have ice enough down here in Virginia to worry about, so they say."

Which was true enough on ordinary occasions. But the frost the night before had been a hard one and the air was still tingling with it. In the shady places the pools remained skimmed over. A gallop over the fields and through the woodland paths put both the horses and riders in a glow of excitement.

Alice B. Emerson

Perhaps Betty was a little careless—at least too confident. Her gray got the lead and sped away across some rough ground which bordered a ravine. Bob shouted again for her to be careful, and Betty turned and waved her hand reassuringly to him.

It was just then that Jim slipped on the edge of the bank. Both of his front feet slid on an icy patch and he almost came to his knees. Betty saved herself from going over his head by a skillful lunge backward, pulling sharply on the reins.

But the horse did not so easily regain his foot-hold. The edge of the bank crumbled. Betty did not utter a sound, but the girls behind her screamed in unison.

"Stop! Wait! She'll be killed!"

Betty knew that Bob was coming at a thundering pace on his brown mount; but the gray horse was on its haunches, sliding down the slope of the ravine, snorting as it went. Betty could not stop her horse, but she clung manfully to the reins and sat back in her saddle as though glued to it.

Just what would happen when they reached the bottom of the slope was a very serious question.

CHAPTER IV

A SECOND IDA BELLETHORNE

The ravine was forty feet deep, and although the path, down which the gray horse slid with Betty Gordon on his back, was of sand and gravel only, there were some boulders and thick brush at the bottom that threatened disaster to both victims of the accident.

Swiftly and more swiftly the frightened horse slid, and the girl had no idea what she should do when they came, bumpy-ti-bump to the bottom.

She heard Bob shouting something to her, but she did not immediately comprehend what he said. Something, she thought it was, about her stirrups. But this was no time or place to look to see if her stirrup leathers were the proper length or if her feet were firmly fixed in the irons, which both Bob and Uncle Dick had warned her about when first she had begun to ride.

Although she dared not look back, Betty knew that Bob had galloped to the very edge of the ravine and had now flung himself from his saddle. She heard his boots slam into the sliding gravel of the hill. He shouted again—that cheery hail that somehow helped Betty to hold on to her fast

Alice B. Emerson

vanishing courage.

"Kick your feet out of the stirrups, Betty!"

What he meant finally seeped into Betty's clouded brain. She realized that Bob Henderson, her chum, the boy she had learned to have such confidence in, was coming down that bank in mighty strides, prepared to save her if it was possible.

The gray horse was struggling and snorting; he was likely to tumble sideways at any moment. If he did, and Betty was caught under him—

But she was not caught in any such crushing pressure. It was Bob's arm around her waist that squeezed her. She had kicked her feet loose of the stirrups, and now Bob, throwing himself backward, tore her out of the saddle. He fell upon his back, and Betty, struggling and laughing and almost crying, fell on top of him.

"All right, Betty! All right!" gasped Bob. "No need to squeal now."

"Who's squealing?" she demanded. "Let me up, do! Are you hurt, Bob?"

"Only the wind knocked out of me. Woof! You all right?"

"Oh, my dear!" shrieked Bobby at the top of the bank. "Are you killed, Betty?"

"Only half killed," gasped Betty. "Don't worry. Spread the news. Elizabeth Gordon, Miss Sharpe's prize Latin scholar, will yet return to Shadyside to make glad the heart of—"

"She's all right," broke in Tommy Tucker, having dismounted and looking over the brink of the bank. "She's trying to be funny. Her neck isn't broken."

"I declare, Tommy!" cried Louise Littell admonishingly, "you sound as though you rather thought her poor little neck ought to be dislocated."

"Cheese!" gasped Teddy, Tommy's twin. "You got that word out of a book, Louise—you know you did."

"So I did; out of the dictionary. There are a lot more of them there, if you want to know," and Louise laughed.

"Oh!" at this point rose a yearning cry. "Oh!" I just think he is too dear for anything!"

"Cracky! What's broke loose now?" demanded Tommy Tucker, jerking back his head to stare all around at the group on the brink of the high bank.

"Who is too expensive, Libbie?" asked Bobby, glancing at her cousin with a look of annoyance displayed in her features.

"Robert Henderson. He is a hero!" gasped the plump girl.

"I know that hero has torn his coat," Louise said, still gazing down into the ravine.

Of course Bob had played a heroic part; but the rest of those present would have considered it almost indecent to speak of it as Libbie did. She continued to clasp her hands and gaze soulfully into the ravine. Bob, having made sure that Betty was all right, had gone down to the bottom of the slope and helped the gray horse to its feet. The animal was more

Alice B. Emerson

frightened than hurt, although its legs were scratched some and it favored one fore foot when Bob walked it about.

"Dear me!" cried Betty, coming closer. "Poor old Jim! Is he hurt much, Bob?"

"I don't believe so," her friend replied.

"Can we get him up the bank?"

"I won't try that if there is any outlet to this ravine—and there must be, of course. Say! do you hear that silly girl?"

"Who? Libbie?" Betty began to giggle. "She is going to make a hero of you, Bob, whether you want to be or not. And you are—"

"Now, don't you begin," growled Bob.

"I never saw such a modest fellow," laughed Betty, giving his free hand a little squeeze.

"Huh! Libbie will want to put a laurel wreath on my brow if I climb up there. See! There is a bunch of laurels right over there—those glossy-leaved, runty sort of trees. Not for me! I am going to lead Jim out ahead, and you climb up, if you want to, and come along with the rest of the bunch. Ride my horse, if you will, Betty."

"So you'd run away from a girl!" scoffed Betty, but laughing. "You are no hero, Bob Henderson."

"Sure I'm not," he agreed cheerfully. "And I'd run away from a girl like Libbie any day. I wonder how Timothy Derby stands for her. But he's almost as mushy as a soft pumpkin!"

With this disrespectful observation Bob started off with the gray horse and Betty scrambled up the bank down which she had plunged so heedlessly.

Bobby was one of those who had dismounted at the brink of the ravine, and she held out a brown hand to Betty as the latter scrambled up the last yard or two of the steep bank and helped her to a secure footing.

"Are you all right, Betty dear?" she cried.

"No. One side of me is left," laughed Betty. "Wasn't that some slide?"

"Now, don't try to make out that you did it on purpose!" exclaimed Esther, the youngest Littell sister.

"It was too lovely for anything," sighed Libbie.

"I'm glad you think so," said Betty. "Oh! you mean what Bob did. I see. Of course he is lovely—always has been. But don't tell him so, for it utterly spoils boys if you praise them— doesn't it Bobby?"

"Of course it does," agreed Betty's particular chum, whose real name, Roberta, was seldom used even by her parents.

"I like that!" chorused the Tucker twins. "Wait till we tell Bob, Betty," added Tommy Tucker, shaking his head.

"If you try to slide downhill on horseback again, we'll all just let you slide to the very bottom," said Teddy.

"Don't fret," returned Betty gaily. "I don't intend to take another such slide—"

Alice B. Emerson

"Not even if your Uncle Dick takes you up to Mountain Camp?" asked Bobby. "There's fine tobogganing up there, he says. Mmmm!"

"Don't talk about it!" wailed Betty. "You know we can't go, for school begins next week and Uncle Dick won't hear to anything breaking in on my schooling."

"Not even measles?" suggested Tommy Tucker solemnly. "Two of the fellows were quarantined with it when we left Salsette," he added.

"Oh! don't speak of such a horrid thing," gasped Libbie, who did not consider measles in the least romantic. "You get all speckled like—like a zebra if you have 'em."

The twins uttered a concerted shout and almost rolled out of their saddles into which they had again mounted after assisting the girls, Betty being astride Bob's horse.

"Speckled like a zebra is good!" Bobby Littell said laughingly to her plump cousin. "I suppose you think a barber's pole is speckled, Libbie?"

These observations attracted the deluded Libbie sufficiently from her hero-worship, so that when Bob Henderson came up out of the ravine to join them a mile beyond the scene of the accident, he was perfectly safe from Libbie's romantic consideration.

The boy and girl friends were then in a deep discussion of the chances, pro and con, of Betty's Uncle Dick taking her with him to Mountain Camp despite the imminent opening of the term at Shadyside.

"Of course there is scarcely a possibility of his doing so,"

Betty said finally with hopeless mien. "Mr. Canary—Uncle Dick's friend is named Jonathan Canary, isn't that a funny name?" she interrupted herself to ask.

"He's a bird," declared Teddy Tucker solemnly.

"Nothing romantic sounding about that name," his brother said, with a look at Libbie. "'Jonathan Canary'—no poetry in that."

"He, he!" chuckled Ted wickedly. "Talking about poetry—"

"But we weren't!" said Bobby Littell. "We were talking about going to Mountain Camp in the Adirondacks. Think of it—in the dead of winter!"

"Talking about poetry," steadily pursued Teddy Tucker. "You know Timothy Derby is always gushing."

"A 'gusher,'" interposed Betty primly, "is an oil well that comes in with a bang."

"Don't you mean it comes out with a bang?" teased Louise.

"In or out, Betty and I have seen 'em gush all right," cried Bob, as they cantered on together along a well-defined bridle-path.

"Say! I'm telling you something," exploded Teddy Tucker, who did not purpose to have his tale lost sight of. "Something about Timothy Derby."

"Oh, dear me, yes!" exclaimed Bobby. "Do tell it and get it over, Ted."

The twins both began to chuckle and Teddy had some

Alice B. Emerson

difficulty in going on with his story. But it seemed they had been at the Derby place the evening before and Timothy had been "boring everybody to distraction," Ted said, reading "Excelsior" to the family.

"And believe me!" interjected Tommy Tucker, "that kid can elocute."

"And he's always been at it," hurried on his twin, giggling. "Here's what Mr. Derby says Timothy recited the first time he ever spoke a piece at a Sunday School concert. You know; the stuff the little mites cackle."

"How elegant are your expressions, Teddy!" remarked Louise, sighing.

But she was amused as well as the others when Ted produced a paper on which he had written down the verse Mr. Derby said his son had recited, and just as Timothy had said it!

"Listen, all of you," begged Teddy. "Now, don't laugh and spoil it all, Tom. Listen:

> "'Lettuce denby uppan doing
> Widow Hartford N E fate,
> Still H E ving, still pursuing,
> Learn to label Aunty Waite.'"

Libbie's voice rose above the general laughter, and she was quite warm. For Libbie's was a loyal soul.

"I don't care! I don't believe it. His father is always making fun of Timothy. He—he is cruel, I think. And, anyway, Timothy was only a little boy then."

"What did he want to label his Aunty Waite for?" demanded Bob.

"You all be pretty good," called Betty, seeing that Libbie was really getting angry. "If you aren't I'll ask Timothy and Libbie to my party at Mountain Camp and none of the rest of you shall go."

"Easy enough said, that, Betty," Bob rejoined. "You haven't very much chance of going there. But, crimpy! wouldn't it be great if Uncle Dick did take us?"

"Remember our school duties, children," drawled Louise. "'Still H E ving, still pursuing.' We must not cry for the moon."

Thus, with a great deal of laughter and good-natured chatter, the cavalcade trotted on and came finally to what Louise and Bobby said was the entrance to Bolter's Farm.

"All our horses were raised on this farm," explained Louise. "Daddy says that Lewis Bolter has the finest stock of any horseman in Virginia. Much of it is racing stock. He sells to the great stables up north. One of his men will know what to do for your gray's scratched legs, Betty."

For Betty had changed with Bob again and rode Jim, the horse that had slid down into the ravine. Betty was really sorry about the scratches and felt somehow as though she were a little to blame for the accident. She should have been more careful in guiding the gray.

Once at the great stables and paddocks, however, Betty's mind was relieved on this point. Louise had an errand from her father to Mr. Bolter and went away with Esther to interview the horse owner. Mr. Littell was a builder and

Alice B. Emerson

constructor and he bought many work horses of Mr. Bolter's raising, as well as saddle stock.

If there was anything on four feet that Betty and Bob loved, it was a horse. In the west they had ridden almost continually; their mounts out at Flame City had been their dearest possessions and they would have been glad to bring them east, both Betty's Clover-pony and Bob's big white horse, had it been wise to do so.

At Shadyside and Salsette, however, there had been no opportunity for horseback riding. They had found pleasure in other forms of outdoor exercise. Now, enabled to view so many beautiful and sleek horses, Betty, as well as Bob and the others, dismounted with delight and entered the long stables.

While her gray was being examined by one of the stablemen, Betty went along a whole row of box stalls by herself, in each of which a horse was standing quietly or moving about. More than one came to thrust a soft muzzle over the door of the stall and with pointed ears and intelligent gaze seemed to ask if the pretty, brown-eyed girl had something nice in her pocket.

"Hi, Miss!" croaked a hoarse voice behind her. "If you want to see a bang-hup 'orse—a real topper—come down 'ere."

Betty turned to see a little crooked man, with one shoulder much higher than the other, who walked a good deal like a crab, sideways. He grinned at her cheerfully in spite of his ugly body and twisted features. He really was a dreadfully homely man, and he was not much taller than Betty herself. He wore a grimy jockey cap, a blue blouse and stained white trousers, and it was quite evident that he was one of the stable helpers.

"This 'ere is the lydy for you to see, Miss," continued the little man eagerly. "She's from old Hengland, Miss. I come with her myself and I've knowed her since she was foaled. Mr. Bolter ain't got in 'is 'ole stable, Miss, a mare like this one."

He pointed to a glossy black creature in the end box. Before the animal raised her head and looked over the gate, Betty knew that the mare from England was one of the most beautiful creatures she had ever seen.

"Hi, now, 'ow's that for a pretty lydy, Miss?" went on the rubber proudly.

"Oh! See! She knows you! Look at the beauty!" gasped Betty, as the black mare reached over the gate and gently nipped the blue sleeve of the crooked little man.

"Knows me? I should sye she does," he said proudly. "Why, she wouldn't take her meals from nobody but me. I told 'em so w'en I 'eard she was sold to Hamerica. And they found Hi was right, Miss, afore hever they got 'er aboard the ship. They sent for me, an' Mr. Bolter gave me a good job with 'er. I goes with Ida Bellethorne wherever she goes. That's the—"

"Ida Bellethorne?" interrupted Betty in amazement

"Yes, Miss. That's 'er nyme. Ida Bellethorne. She comes of the true Bellethorne stock. The last of the breed out o' the Bellethorne stables, Miss."

"Ida Bellethorne!" exclaimed Betty again. "Isn't that odd? A horse and a girl of the same name!"

But this last she did not say audibly. The cockney rubber was fondling the mare's muzzle and he did not hear Betty's

Alice B. Emerson

comment. The discovery of this second Ida Bellethorne excited Betty enormously.

CHAPTER V

MEASLES

Betty Gordon's active mind could not let this incident pass without further investigation. Not alone was she interested in the beautiful black mare and the girl in the neighborhood shop, but she wanted to know how they came to have the same name.

Betty was a practical girl. Bob often said it was not easy to fool Betty. She had just as strong an imagination as any other girl of her age and loved to weave fancies in her own mind when it was otherwise idle. But she knew her dreams were dreams, and her imaginings unreal.

It struck her that the name "Ida Bellethorne" was more suitable for a horse than for a girl. Betty wondered all in a flash if the English girl who had sold her the silk sweater in the neighborhood shop that morning and who confessed that she had come from England practically alone had not chosen this rather resounding name to use as an alias. Perhaps she had run away from her friends and was hiding her identity behind the name of a horse that she had heard of as being famous on the English turf.

This was not a very hard thing for Betty to imagine. And, in

Alice B. Emerson

any case, her interest was stirred greatly by the discovery she had made. She was about to speak to the little, crooked man regarding the name when something occurred to draw her attention from the point of her first surprise.

The mare, Ida Bellethorne, coughed. She coughed twice.

"Ah-ha, my lydy!" exclaimed the rubber, shaking his head and stepping away from the door of the stall that the mare should not muzzle his clothing. "That's a fine sound—wot?"

"Is it dust in her poor nose?" asked the interested Betty.

"'Tis worse nor dust. 'Tis wot they call 'ere the 'orse distemper, Miss. You tyke it from 'Unches Slattery, the change in climate and crossin' the hocean ain't done Ida Bellethorne a mite of good."

"Is that your name? 'Hunches Slattery'?" Betty asked curiously.

"That's wot they've called me this ten year back. You see, I was a jockey when I was a lad, and a good one, too, if Hi do say it as shouldn't. But I got throwed in a steeplechase race. When they let me out o' the 'orspital I was like this—'unchbacked and crooked. I been 'Unchie ever since, Miss."

"I am so sorry," breathed Betty Gordon softly.

But the crooked little rubber was more interested in Ida Bellethorne's history than he was in his own misfortune, which was an old story.

"I was working in the Bellethorne stables when this mare was foaled. I was always let work about her. She's a wonnerful pedigree, Miss—aw, yes, wonnerful! And she was named for an 'igh and mighty lydy, sure enough."

"Named for a lady?" cried Betty. "Don't you mean for a girl?"

"Aw, not much! Such a lydy, Miss! Fine, an' tall, and wonnerful to look at. They said she could sing like a hangel, that she could. Miss Ida Bellethorne, she was. She ought've been a lord's daughter, she ought."

"What became of her?" asked the puzzled Betty.

"I don't know, Miss. I don't rightly know what became of all the family. I kept close to the mare 'ere; the family didn't so much bother me. But there was trouble and ruin and separation and death; and, after all," added the rubber in a lower tone, "for all I know, there was cheating and swindling of the fatherless and orphan, too. But me, I kept close to this lydy 'ere," and he fondled the mare's muzzle again.

"It's quite wonderful," admitted Betty. But what seemed wonderful to her, the stableman did not know anything about. "I suppose the pretty mare is worth a lot of money?"

"Hi don't know wot Mr. Bolter would sell 'er for, if at all. But 'e paid four thousand pun, laid down at the stables where she was kep' after the smash of the Bellethorne family. She's got a pedigree longer than some lord's families, and 'er track record was what brought Mr. Lewis Bolter to Hengland when she was quietly put on the market.

"Maybe they couldn't 'ave sold 'er to Henglish turfman," he added, whispering softly in Betty's ear, "for maybe the title to 'er would be clouded hand if she won another race somebody might go into court about it."

Betty did not understand this; and just then the mare began to cough again and she was troubled by Ida Bellethorne's condition.

"Is that the black mare, Slattery?" demanded a voice behind them.

"Yes, sir," said the crooked little man respectfully, touching his cap.

Betty turned to see a gentleman in riding boots and a short coat with a dog-whip in his gloved hand, whom she believed at once to be Mr. Bolter. Nor was she mistaken.

"She's a beauty, isn't she, my dear?" the horseman said kindly. "But I do not like that cough. I've made up my mind, Slattery. She goes to-morrow to Cliffdale, and of course you go with her. Pack your bag to-night. I have already tele-phoned for a stable-car to be on the siding in the morning."

"Yes, sir. Wot she needs is dry hair, an' the 'igher the better," said the crooked man, nodding.

"They will put her on her feet again," agreed Mr. Bolter. "The balsam air around Cliffdale is the right lung-healer for man or beast."

He went out and Betty heard the girls calling to her. She thanked Hunchie Slattery, patted Ida Bellethorne's nose, and ran out of the stable.

But her head was full of the mystery of the striking name of "Ida Bellethorne." She felt she must tell somebody, and Bobby of course, who was her very closest chum, must be the recipient of her story as the cavalcade started homeward. It was Bobby whom Betty wanted to have the blue blouse just as soon as the shopgirl finished it.

"Now, what do you think of that?" Betty demanded, after she had delivered, almost in a breath, a rather garbled story of the strange girl and the black mare from England.

"Goodness, Betty, how wonderful!" exclaimed her friend. "I do so want to see that over-blouse you bought. And you say she is making another?"

"Is that all you've got to say about it?" demanded Betty, staring.

"Why—er—you know, it really is none of our business, is it?" asked Bobby, but with dancing eyes. "You know Miss Prettyman told us that the greatest fault of character under which young ladies labor to-day is vulgar curiosity. Oh, my! I can see her say it now," declared naughty Bobby, shaking her head.

"But, Bobby! Do think a bit! A girl and a horse both of the same name, and just recently from England! I'm going to ask right out what it means."

"Who are you going to ask—the horse?" giggled Bobby.

"Oh, you! No, I can't ask the pretty black mare," Betty said, shaking her head. "For she is going to be sent away for her health. She's got what they call 'distemper.' She has to be acclimated, or something."

"It sounds as though it might hurt," observed Bobby gravely.

"Something ought to hurt you," said Betty laughing. "You are forever and ever poking fun. But I am going to see Ida Bellethorne in the shop and find out what she knows about

Alice B. Emerson

the pretty mare."

"Well, I'm sorry I didn't see the horse," confessed Bobby. "But I'll go with you to see the girl. And I do want to see the blouse."

That, Betty showed her the moment they arrived at Fairfields and could run upstairs to the room the two girls shared while Betty visited here. The latter unfolded the orange-silk blouse and spread it on the bed. Bobby went into exstacies over it, as in duty bound.

"Wait till you see the one she is making for you," Betty said. "You'll love it!"

"What is that you are going to love?" asked a voice outside the open door. "Measles?"

"Oh, Bob! Who ever heard the like?" demanded Betty. "Love measles, indeed. Why—What makes you look so queer?"

"Greatest thing you ever heard, girls!" cried Bob, his face very red and his eyes shining. "I didn't really understand how much I had come to hate books and drill these last few weeks."

"What do you mean?" demanded Roberta Littell. "If you don't tell us at once!"

"Why, didn't you hear? Telegrams have come. To all our parents and guardians. Measles! Measles! Measles!"

He began to dance a very poor imitation of the Highland Fling in the hall. The girls ran out and seized him, one on either side, and big as Bob was they managed to shake him soundly.

"Tell us what you mean!" commanded Betty.

"Who has the measles?" cried Bobby.

"Everybody! Or, pretty near everybody, I guess. The chaps who had it and were quarantined when we came away from Salsette, gave it to the servants. And it has spread to the village. And Miss Prettyman's got it and a lot of the other folks at Shadyside. Oh, my eye!"

"Are you fooling us, Bob?" demanded Betty.

"Honor bright! It is just as I say. Of course, it all isn't in the messages the two schools have sent out to 'parents and guardians.' That is the way the messages are headed, you know. But the Shadyside *Mirror* has come, too, and tells all about it. Opening is postponed for a fortnight. What do you know about that?" and Bob began his clumsy dance again.

Betty broke away and darted down the stairs. She scarcely touched the steps with her feet she flew so fast, and if it had not been for the banister she surely would have come to the bottom in a heap.

She ran out on the porch to find her Uncle Dick smoking a cigar and reading the paper in a warm corner. Like a stone from a catapult she flung herself into his arms.

"Oh, Uncle Dick! Uncle Dick! Now we can go!" she cried, seizing him tightly around the neck.

"Goodness, child!" choked Uncle Dick, fairly throttled by her exuberance. "What is it? Go where, Betty?"

"To Mountain Camp! With you! All of us! No school for more than two weeks! Oh, Uncle Dick!" Then she suddenly stopped and her glowing face lost its color and her excitement subsided. "Dear me!" she quavered, "I 'member now I had 'em when I was six, and they say you can't have 'em but once."

"What can't you have but once?"

"Measles," said Betty, sighing deeply. "I suppose after all I can go back to Shadyside. Maybe Mrs. Eustice will expect all of us that have had 'em to come."

CHAPTER VI

A DISAPPEARANCE

There was an exciting conclave at Fairfields that evening. Perhaps I should say two. For in one room given over by the good-natured Mrs. Littell to the young folks there was a most noisy conclave while the older members of the household held a more quiet if no less earnest conference in the library.

There were eight in the young folks' meeting for Mrs. Littell insisted upon Esther's going to bed at a certain hour every evening "to get her beauty sleep."

"And I'll say she is sure to be a raving beauty when she grows up, if she keeps going to bed with the chickens," giggled Bobby.

"You know she can't go to Mountain Camp anyway," Louise said quietly, "for her school isn't measly and it begins again day after to-morrow."

"Poor Esther!" sighed Betty. "We must make it up to her somehow. I was afraid she would cry at dinner this evening."

"She's a good kid," agreed Bobby. "But are you sure, Betty, that we can go to the mountains? Just think! Eight of us!"

Alice B. Emerson

"Some contract for Mr. Gordon," observed Tommy Tucker with unusual reflection.

"How about it's being some contract for Mr. and Mrs. Canary?" suggested Bob Henderson. "Maybe they will shy at such a crowd."

"I asked Uncle Dick about that," Betty said eagerly. "He told me all about Mr. and Mrs. Canary. He has known them for years and years. They must be awfully nice people and they have got a great, big, rambling bungalow sort of house, all built of logs in the rough. But inside there is a heating plant, and electric lights, and shower baths, and everything up-to-date. Mr. Canary is very wealthy; but his money could not keep him from getting tuber—tuber—"

"'Tubers,'" said Bob with gravity, "are potatoes, or something of that kind."

"Now, Bob! you know what I mean very well," cried Betty. "His lungs were affected. But they have healed and he is perfectly well as long as he stays up there in the wilderness. The air there has wonderful cur—curative properties. There!"

"Look! Will it cure such a bad attack of poetry?" interrupted Bobby, drawing the attention of the others to Timothy Derby and Libbie who, with heads close together, were absorbed in a volume of verses the boy had brought with him from home.

"It might help," said Bob. "It ought to be cold enough up there at Mountain Camp to freeze romance into an icicle."

"I hope we all go then," Teddy Tucker agreed. "Our folks have said we could—haven't they, Tom?"

"With suspicious alacrity," agreed his twin. "How's that for a fine phrase, Louise? Do you know, I think mother and dad were almost shocked when they got the telegram from Salsette and knew our vacation was to be prolonged. The idea of Mountain Camp seems to please them."

"Goodness! I know dear Mrs. Littell doesn't feel that way about it," cried Betty.

"She's got girls," said Ted dryly. "You know it is us boys who are not appreciated in this world."

"Yes," said Bob, "you fellows are terribly abused, I'll say. But, now! Are we all sure of going? That's what I want to know."

"Timothy—" began Louise; but Bob held up his hand to stop her.

"I know from his father that Tim can go. Uncle Dick is sure to take us, Betty, isn't he?"

"He sent off a telegram to Mrs. Canary this evening. If she sends back word 'Yes' we can go day after to-morrow."

"That's all right then," said Bob, quite as eagerly. 'The thing to do then is to plan what to take and all that. It is cold up there, but dry. Much colder than it was at school before we came down. Furs, overcoats, boots, mittens—not gloves, for gloves are no good when it is really cold—and underthings that are warm and heavy. We don't want to come back with noses and toes frozen off."

"Humph!" said Bobby scornfully, "what kind of underwear should you advise our getting for our noses, Bob Henderson?"

Alice B. Emerson

"Aw—you know what I mean," said the boy, grinning. "Don't depend on a fur piece around your neck and a muff to keep the rest of you warm. Us fellows have all got Mackinaws and boots and such things. And we'll want 'em."

And so they excitedly made their plans. At least, six of them did while Timothy and Libbie bent their minds upon the book. One thing about those two young romanticists, they agreed to the plans the others made and were quite docile.

At ten Timothy and the Tucker twins went home and the others went cheerfully up to bed. While Betty Gordon remained at Fairfields Bobby insisted on sharing her own room with her. They were never separated at Shadyside, so why should they be here?

When she was half undressed Betty suddenly went down on her knees before the tall chiffonier and opened the lower drawer. She dug under everything in the drawer until she came to her handbag, and drew it forth.

"I declare!" chuckled Bobby, "I thought you were digging a new burrow like a homeless rabbit. What did you forget?"

"Didn't forget anything," responded Betty, smiling up at her friend. "I remembered something."

"Oh!"

"My locket. Uncle Dick's present. I wanted to see that it was safe."

"Goodness! Do you carry it in your bag?"

"I've got a lovely chain at Shadyside, you know. I told Uncle Dick not to buy a chain. And I don't believe Mrs. Eustice will object to a simple little locket like mine, will she?"

"M-m-m! I don't know," replied Bobby. "You know she is awfully opposed to us girls wearing jewelry. And your locket is lovely. Just think! Platinum and a real diamond. Why! what is the matter, Betty?"

For Betty had begun scrambling in her bag worse than she had in the bureau drawer. Everything came out—purse, tickets, gloves, handkerchief, the tiniest little looking-glass, a letter or two, a silver thimble, two coughdrops stuck together, a sample of ribbon which she had failed to match, a most disreputable looking piece of lead-pencil—

But no twist of tissue paper with the locket in it!

"What is the matter?" repeated Bobby, frightened by the expression of the other girl's face.

"I—I—Oh, Bobby! It's gone!" wailed Betty.

"Not your locket?"

"Yes, my locket!" sobbed Betty, and she sat down on the floor and wept.

"Why, it can't be! Who would take it? When did you see it last? Nobody here in the house would have stolen it, Betty."

"It—it must have dropped out of my bag. Oh! what shall I do? I can't tell Uncle Dick."

"He won't punish you for losing it, will he?"

"But think how he'll feel! And how I'll feel!" wailed Betty. "He advised me to put it somewhere for safe keeping until I

Alice B. Emerson

got my chain. And I wouldn't. I—I wanted it with me."

"You should have put it downstairs in daddy's safe," said Bobby thoughtfully.

"But that doesn't do me a bit of good now," sobbed Betty Gordon.

"Don't you remember where you had it last?" asked her friend slowly.

"In my bag, of course. And I carried my bag to town to-day. Yes! I remember seeing the paper it was in at the bottom of my bag more than once while I was shopping. Oh, dear! what shall I do?"

"Then you are quite sure it was not stolen?" Bobby suggested.

"No. I don't suppose it was. It just hopped out somehow. But where? That is the question, Bobby. I can't answer it."

She rose finally and finished her preparations for bed. Bobby was very sympathetic; but there did not seem to be anything she could say that would really relieve Betty's heart, or help in any way. The locket was gone and no trace of how it had gone had been left in Betty's mind.

When the light was out Bobby crept into Betty's bed and held her tightly in her arms.

"Don't cry, Betty dear!" the other girl whispered. "Maybe your Uncle Dick will know how to find the locket."

"Oh, Bobby! I can't tell him. I'm ashamed to," sighed Betty. "It looks as though I had not cared enough about his present to be careful with it. And I thought if I carried it about with me that there would be no chance of my losing it. And now—"

"Then tell Bob," suggested her chum, hugging Betty tightly.

"Bob?"

"Tell him all about it," said Bobby Littell. "Perhaps he will know what to do. You can't really have lost that beautiful locket forever, Betty!"

"Oh, I don't know! It's gone, anyway!" sobbed Betty.

"Don't give up. That isn't like you, Betty," went on Bobby. "Maybe Bob can help. We can ask him, at least."

"Yes, we can do that," was Betty's not very hopeful reply.

Alice B. Emerson

CHAPTER VII

ALL MRS. STAPLES COULD SAY

The two girls sought out Bob Henderson before breakfast and told him of the disappearance of Betty's beautiful little locket. Betty's eyes, were a little swollen and even Bobby seemed not to have passed a very agreeable night. Bob was quite shrewd enough to see these evidences of trouble and he refrained from making any remark even in fun to ruffle the girls.

"Here's a pretty mess!" exclaimed Bob, but cheerfully. "And we all going to Mountain Camp to-morrow if Mrs. Canary telegraphs 'Yes,' Hunted everywhere, I suppose?"

"Yes, Bob," Betty assured him. "And there was but one place to hunt. In my bag."

"Sure?"

"Pos-i-tive!"

"Carried it loose in your bag, did you?" he asked reflectively.

"Wrapped up in white tissue paper. You know, the box it came in got broken."

"I remember. Gee, Betty! that's an awfully pretty locket. You don't want to lose it."

"But I have lost it!"

"For keeps, I mean," rejoined Bob, smiling encouragingly. "Come on! Let's see the bag. Where did you carry it? When was the last time you saw the locket in the bag and where?"

"Oh!" Betty cried suddenly. "I remember it was in the bag when I was shopping yesterday."

"Shopping where? Let's hear about the last place you remember seeing it."

Betty remembered very clearly seeing the twist of paper with the locket in it while she was at Purcell's where she had bought some veiling.

"Then, Betty," said Bobby, "you went to that little store afterward, you said, where you got the over-blouse."

"Ye—es. But I didn't notice it while I was there. I was so excited over the blouse and so interested in Ida Bellethorne that I don't remember of looking in my bag to see if my locket was safe."

"'Ida Bellethorne'?" repeated Bob in surprise. "Why! that's the name of Mr. Lewis Bolter's new mare from England. I heard Mr. Littell and Uncle Dick talking about her."

"And I met a girl named Ida Bellethorne. I'll tell you all about her later, Bob," said Betty. "Just now I want to know what to do about the locket."

"I should say you did! And I'll tell you what," Bob said

Alice B. Emerson

promptly. "Right after breakfast we'll borrow the little car and I'll take you over to Georgetown and we'll go to every place you went to yesterday, Betty, and inquire. I'm allowed to drive in the District of Columbia, you know."

"Will you, Bob?" cried Betty. "Do you think there is any chance of our finding it?"

"Why not? If it was picked up in one of the stores you went to. There are lots more honest people in the world than there are dishonest. Come on now, don't cry."

"I'm not going to cry," declared Betty. "I've cried enough already. Don't tell the others, Bob. Nor Uncle Dick. I don't want him to know if I can help it. It looks just as though I didn't prize his present enough to take care of it."

Somehow, Betty felt encouraged by Bob's taking hold of the matter. The small car was secured after breakfast and Bob and the two girls set off for the other side of the river. It was not alone because of Bob's advice that they stopped first at the little neighborhood shop on the hilly side street where Betty had bought her sweater. Bobby was anxious to see her blue sweater, and the two girls ran in as soon as the car halted before the door.

The little bell over it jingled pleasantly at their entrance; but it was a tall and rather grim-looking woman who came from the back of the shop to meet them instead of the English girl with whom Betty had dealt on her former visit.

"Humph!" said Mrs. Staples, for it was she, when she spied the over-blouse under Betty's coat. "You are the young lady who was to purchase the blue blouse when it was finished?"

"For my friend here," said Betty, bringing Bobby forward. "I know she will like it."

"I hope so," said Mrs. Staples. "It is finished. Ida sat up most of the night to finish it. Here it is," and she displayed the dark blue blouse for the girls to see.

"How lovely!" ejaculated Bobby eagerly. "I like it even better than I do your orange one, Betty. It's sweet."

"It's twelve dollars, Miss," said the shop woman promptly. "You can pay me and take the blouse. I paid Ida for it."

"Isn't the girl who made it here?" asked Betty anxiously.

"No, she ain't," said Mrs. Staples in her blunt way. "She left an hour ago."

"Oh! Will she come back?"

"I don't expect her. I am sure I cannot be changing help all the time. She left me very abruptly. I did not ask her to come back."

"Why," said Betty, wonderingly, "I thought you were her friend. Isn't she all alone in this country?"

"She is a girl who seems quite able to take care of herself," the grim shopwoman said. "Or she is determined to try. I advised her to write to her aunt—"

"Then she has an aunt over here?" cried Betty eagerly.

"So she thinks. An aunt for whom Ida was named. There was some family trouble, and Ida's father and her father's sister seem to have had nothing to do with each other for some years. The aunt is a singer—quite a noted concert singer, it

Alice B. Emerson

seems. Ida came to Washington expecting to find her. She did not find the elder Ida Bellethorne—"

"Then there are three Ida Bellethornes!" whispered Bobby in Betty's ear.

"So she came here to help me," continued Mrs. Staples, all the time watching Betty with a rather strange manner. "She would better have remained with me, as I told her. But she found in the paper last night this notice," the woman produced a torn piece of paper from the counter and handed it to Betty, "and nothing would do but Ida must go right away to find the place and the person mentioned here."

The two girls in great interest bent their heads above the piece of paper. The marked paragraph was one of several in the column and read as follows:

"It is stated upon good authority that the great Ida Bellethorne will arrive at Cliffdale, New York, within a day or two, and will remain for the winter."

"Why, how odd," murmured Betty. "And did this make Ida go away?"

"She has gone to Cliffdale to meet her aunt. That was her intention," said Mrs. Staples. "Are either of you young ladies prepared to buy this blue blouse?"

"Oh, yes, indeed!" cried Bobby, who had taken a fancy to the blouse. "I've got money enough. And it was nice of Miss Bellethorne to finish it for me before she went. I wish I might thank her personally."

"I do not expect to see Ida again," the shopwoman repeated in her most severe manner, wrapping up the over-blouse.

"Twelve dollars—thank you, Miss. Can I show you anything else?"

"Wait!" gasped Betty. "I want to ask you—I wanted to ask Ida Bellethorne if she saw me drop anything here in the store yesterday?"

"I am sorry she is not here to answer that question," said Mrs. Staples. "I was not here when you came, Miss."

"No, I know you weren't. But somewhere while I was shopping yesterday I lost something out of my bag. If it dropped out here—"

"I can assure you I picked up nothing, Miss," declared the shop woman.

"If Ida—"

"If Ida Bellethorne did, she is not here, unfortunately, to tell you," said Mrs. Staples in her same manner and without a change of expression on her hard face.

"Oh, dear!" sighed Betty.

"But you don't know that you dropped it here," Bobby said to encourage her. But perhaps it encouraged Mrs. Staples more!

"I have nothing more to say, Miss," the woman declared. "Ida not being here—"

"Oh, well," said Betty, trying to speak more cheerfully, "it is true I do not remember having seen it while I was here at all. So—so we will go to the other places. Of course, if Ida had found anything she would have told you?"

"I cannot be responsible for what Ida Bellethorne would do or say," replied the shopwoman grimly. "Not having been here myself when you came, Miss—"

"Oh, yes! I understand," said Betty hastily. "Well, thank you for keeping the blouse for us. Good-bye."

She and Bobby were not greatly pleased with Mrs. Staples. But they had no reason for distrusting her. When they had gone the shopwoman smiled a most wintry smile.

"Well, I am not supposed to tell people how to go about their own affairs, I should hope," was her thought. "That chit never told me what she had lost. It might have been a pair of shoes or a boiled lobster! Humph! Folks would better speak plain in this world. I always do, I am sure."

CHAPTER VIII

UNCLE DICK MUST BE TOLD

The two girls did not tell Bob Henderson all that had happened in the little shop when they first came out. They were in too much haste to get to the other places where it might be possible that Betty had dropped her locket. Of all things, they did not suspect that Mrs. Staples knew the first thing about it.

But they did tell the boy that Ida Bellethorne had gone away.

"Where's she gone?" asked the inquisitive Bob. "Couldn't be that she found the locket and ran off with it?"

"Why, you're almost horrid!" declared Betty, aggrieved. "You don't know what a nice girl Ida is."

"Humph!" (Could he have caught that expression from waiting outside Mrs. Staples' shop?) "Humph! I don't believe you know how nice she is, or otherwise. You never saw her but once."

"But she's seen the horse," giggled Bobby.

"What horse?" demanded Bob.

Alice B. Emerson

"Mr. Lewis Bolter's black mare, Ida Bellethorne."

"Oh!"

"And, oh, Bob!" cried Betty, "there's another Ida Bellethorne, and this Ida has gone away to see her. She's her aunt."

"Who's her aunt?" grumbled Bob, who was having some difficulty just then in driving the car and so could not give his full attention to the matter the girls were chattering about.

"Why, see!" cried Betty, rummaging in her bag. "Here's the piece of newspaper with the society item, or whatever it is, in it that made Ida go away so suddenly this morning. It's about her aunt, the great concert singer. Ida's gone to meet her where that says," and she put the piece of paper into Bob's hand.

"All right," he said. "Here's Markham and Boggs' place. You said you were in this store yesterday, Betty."

"So I was. Come on, Bobby," cried the other girl, hopping out of the car. "I suppose we shall have to go to the manager or the superintendent or somebody. Dear me! if we don't find my locket I don't know what I shall do."

When Betty and Bobby came out of the store, much disappointed, they found Bob grinning—as Bobby declared—"like a Cheshire cat."

"But never mind the cat," continued Bobby. "What is the matter with that boy? For boys will laugh at the most serious things. And this is serious, my poor, dear Betty."

"Indeed it is," agreed her friend, and so they crossed the walk to the grinning Bob Henderson who had the scrap of newspaper Betty had given him in his hand.

"Say," he drawled, "who did you say this aunt of Ida Bellethorne is?"

"Mrs. Staples says she is a concert singer—a prima donna," replied Betty.

"She's a prima donna all right," chuckled Bob. "Where now? Oh! To Stone's shoe shop? Well, what do you know about this notice in the paper?" and his smile grew broader.

"What do you mean, Bob?" demanded Betty, rather vexed. "You can read the paragraph yourself. 'The great Ida Bellethorne'. That means she is a great singer of course."

"Yes, I see," replied Bob, giving some attention to the steering of the car. "But there is one thing about you girls—you never read the sporting page of the newspaper."

"What is that?" gasped Bobby Littell.

"This string of items you handed me is torn out of the sporting page. All the paragraphs refer to racing matters. That particular one deals with Mr. Bolter's black mare, Ida Bellethorne. Cliffdale is the place he was shipping her to far her health."

"Never!" cried Bobby.

"Oh, Bob! Is that so?" gasped Betty.

Bob burst into open laughter. "That's a good one on you and on your friend, Ida," he declared. "If she has gone to meet her aunt up in New York State she'll meet a horse instead.

Alice B. Emerson

How's that for a joke?"

Betty Gordon shook her head without smiling. "I don't see the joke at all," she said. "Poor Ida! She will be sadly disappointed. And she has lost her position here with Mrs. Staples. We could see that Mrs. Staples was angry because she went away."

"Why," cried Bobby, likewise sympathetic, "I think it is horrid—actually horrid! You needn't laugh, Bob Henderson."

"Shucks!" returned the boy. "I can't cry over it, can I? Of course it is too bad the girl has made such a mistake. But our weeping won't help her."

"No," confessed Bobby, "I suppose that is so."

"And our weeping won't find my locket," sighed Betty. "Dear me! If I did drop it in Stone's place I hope they have saved it for me."

But the locket was not to be found in that shop, either. Nor in the two others which Betty Gordon had visited the previous day. This indeed was a perfectly dreadful thing! The plainer it was that the locket could not be found, the more repentent and distracted Betty became.

"I shall have to tell Uncle Dick—I shall have to," she wailed, when Bob drove them away from the last place and all hope was gone glimmering. "Oh, dear! It is dreadful."

"Don't take on so, Betty!" Bob begged gruffly, for he could not bear to see the girl actually cry. "I'll tell him if you are afraid to."

"Don't you dare!" she flared out at him. "I'm not afraid. Only

I dread it. It was the nicest present he ever gave me and—and I loved it. But I did not take proper care of it. I realize that now, when it is too late."

Bob remained serious of aspect after that. That his mind was engaged with the problem of Betty's lost trinket was proved by what he said on the way back to Fairfields:

"I suppose you spoke to all the clerks you traded with in those stores, Betty?"

"Why, yes. All but Ida Bellethorne, Bob."

"And Mrs. Staples said she didn't know anything about Betty's locket," Bobby put in.

Of course, this was not so; but Bobby thought she was telling the exact truth. The two girls really had not explained Betty's loss to Mrs. Staples at all.

"The English girl going off so suddenly, and on such a wild-goose chase, looks kind of fishy, you know," drawled Bob.

"She thinks she is chasing her aunt!" Bobby cried.

"Maybe."

"You don't even know her, Bob," declared Betty haughtily. "You can't judge her character. I am sure she is honest."

"Well," grumbled Bob, "being sure everybody is honest isn't going to get you that locket back, believe me!"

"That's horrid, too! Isn't it, Betty?" demanded Bobby.

"It's sort of, I guess," said Betty, much troubled, "But, oh,

Alice B. Emerson

Bob! I don't want to think that poor girl found my locket and ran away with it. No, I don't want to believe that. And, anyway, it doesn't help me out a mite. I've got to tell Uncle Dick before he notices that I don't display his pretty present any more. Oh, dear!"

"It's a shame," groaned Bobby, holding her chum's hand tightly.

"Guess there are worse things than measles in this world," observed Bob, as he stopped the small car under the *porte cochere* at Fairfields.

CHAPTER IX

THE LIVE WIRE OCTETTE

It was not an easy thing to do; but Betty Gordon did it. She confessed the whole wretched thing to Uncle Dick and was assured of his forgiveness. But perhaps his serious forgiveness was not the easiest thing for the girl to bear.

"I am sure, as you say, that you did not mean to be careless," Mr. Richard Gordon said gently. It was hard for him to be strict with Betty; but he knew her impulsiveness sometimes led her into a reckless path. "But mark you, Betty: The value of that locket should have, in itself, made you particularly careful of it."

"I—I valued it more because you gave it to me, Uncle Dick," she sobbed.

"And yet that did not make you particularly careful," the gentleman reminded her. "The main trouble with you, Betty, is that you have no very clear appreciation of the value of money."

"Oh, Uncle Dick!" and she looked at him with trembling chin and tears welling into her eyes.

Alice B. Emerson

"And why should you?" he added, laughing more lightly and patting her hand. "You have never been obliged to earn money. Think back to the time you were with the Peabodys. The money my lawyer sent you for your own use just burned holes in your pinafore pockets, didn't it?"

"I didn't wear pinafores, Uncle Dick," Betty said soberly. "Girls don't nowadays."

"No, I see they don't," he rejoined, smiling broadly again. "But they did in my day. However, in whatever pocket you put that money as you got it, the hole was figuratively burned, wasn't it?"

"We—ell, it went mostly for food. Mr. Peabody was such a miser! And—and—"

"And so when you wanted to come away from Bramble Farm you actually had to borrow money," went on Uncle Dick. "Of course, you were fortunate enough finally to get the lawyer's check and pay your debts. But the fact remains that you seem unable to keep money."

"Oh, Uncle Dick!"

"Now," continued her guardian still soberly, "a miser like Mr. Peabody for instance is a very unpleasant person. But a spendthrift often does even more harm in the world than a miser. I don't want my Betty-girl to be a spendthrift."

"Oh, Uncle Dick!"

"The loss of your pretty locket, my dear, has come because of that trait in your character which ignores a proper appreciation of the value of money and what can be bought with it. Now, I can buy you another locket—"

"No, no, Uncle Dick! I don't deserve it," she said with her face hidden against his shoulder as she sat in his lap.

"That is true, my dear. I don't really think you do deserve another—not right at once. And, anyway, we will advertise for the locket in the newspapers and may recover it in that way. So we will postpone the purchase of any other piece of jewelry at present.

"What I have in my mind, however, and have had for some time, is the reorganization of your financial affairs," and now he smiled broadly as she raised her head to look at him. "I think of putting you on a monthly allowance of pocket money and asking you to keep a fairly exact account of your expenditures. Not an account to show me. I don't want you to feel as though you were being watched."

"What do you mean, Uncle Dick?"

"I want you to keep account for your own satisfaction. I want you to know at the end of the month where your money has gone to. It is the best training in the world for a girl, as well as a boy, to know just what she has done with the money that has passed through her hands. And in this case I am sure in time that it will give you a just comprehension of money's value.

"If we do not recover the locket, why, in time, we will look about for another pretty trinket—"

"No, Uncle Dick," Betty said seriously. "I loved that locket. I should have been more careful of it. I hope it will be found and returned to me. I do! I do! But I don't want you to give me another."

"Why not?" he asked, yet giving her quite an understanding look.

Alice B. Emerson

"I guess you know, Uncle Dick," she sighed. "I don't really deserve it. And it wouldn't be that locket that you gave me for Christmas, you see."

"Well, my dear—"

"Wait, dear Uncle Dick! I want to say something more," said the girl, hugging him tightly again. "If you give me a certain sum of money to spend for myself every month I am going to save out of it until I have enough to buy a locket exactly like that one I lost—If it isn't found, I mean."

"Ah!"

"You approve, Uncle Dick?"

"Most assuredly. That would be following out my suggestion of learning to take care of money in the fullest sense, my dear."

"Then," said Betty, bouncing happily on his knee, "that is what I am going to try to do. But I do hope my locket will be found!"

This serious conference was broken up at this point by the arrival of the telegram Uncle Dick had been expecting from Mountain Camp. Mrs. Jonathan Canary had signed it herself and it was to the effect that the young friends of Mr. Richard Gordon would be as welcome as that gentleman himself.

Bob immediately saddled a horse and galloped to the Derbys and the Tuckers to carry the news. Final plans were made for departure the next morning and in spite of a rather threatening change in the weather the party left Fairfields on time and in high spirits for upper New York State.

A few flakes of snow had begun fluttering down as the train pulled out of Washington; and as it raced across the Maryland fields and through the hills which grace that State the snow blew faster and faster and thicker and thicker. But even in midwinter snow storms do not much obstruct traffic so far south, and the gay party from Fairfields had no suspicion that it was being borne into any peril or trouble. What was a little snow which scarcely, at first, caught upon the brown fields?

They had engaged two whole sections for the young folks and an extra place for Uncle Dick. The latter did not interfere at all with the fun and frolic of his charges. He was—he should have been—used by now to the ridiculous antics of the Tucker twins and the overflowing spirits of the rest of the octette. Bachelor as he was, Mr. Richard Gordon considered himself pretty well acquainted with young folks of their age.

The two sections occupied by the eight girls and boys were opposite each other and they had that end of the car pretty much to themselves. Of course, people sometimes had to go through the aisle—and others besides the conductor and the porter; but after running the gauntlet of that lively troop once the restless passenger usually tried to keep out of the "line of fire."

The fun the party had was good-natured sport for the most part. Their practical jokes were aimed at each other rather than at their fellow passengers. But it was a fact that there was very little peace for a nervous person in that Pullman coach.

"We're the live-wire octette, and we are going to let everybody know it," proclaimed Tommy Tucker vociferously. "Say! there's a chap up at the other end of the car, sprawled all over his seat—fresh kid, he is. Did you notice him?"

Alice B. Emerson

"I did," replied his twin. "I fell over his foot twice when I went for a drink."

"Why didn't you look where you were walking?" grinned Bob Henderson craning his neck to see up the aisle and mark the passenger in question.

"Huh!" grumbled Ted, "he stuck it out for me to tumble over both times—and you know this train is joggling some."

"Ill say so," agreed Bob.

But Betty had jumped up to look and she said eagerly:

"Do you mean the man with the silk handkerchief over his head? He must be asleep, or trying to sleep."

"I tell you he is just a fresh kid," said Tommy Tucker. "And I'm going to fix him."

"Now, boys, be careful what you do," advised Louise, who occasionally considered it her duty to put on a sober, admonishing air.

Tommy, however, started for the nearest exit to the platform of the car. He was gone some time, and when he reappeared he carried in both hands a great soggy snowball, bigger than the biggest grapefruit.

"Gee, folks!" he whispered, "it's snowing, and then some! I never saw such a snow. And the porter says it is likely to get worse the farther north we go. Suppose we should be snowbound?"

There was a chorus of cries—of fearful delight on the part of the girls, at least—at this announcement.

"Never mind," Bob Henderson said, "we have a dining car hitched to this train, so we sha'n't starve I guess, if we are snowed up. What are you going to do with that snow, Tommy?"

The Tucker twin winked prodigiously. "I'm going to take it up the aisle and show it to Mr. Gordon. He doesn't know it's snowing like this," said the boy quite soberly.

"Why, Tommy Tucker!" cried Betty, "of course Uncle Dick knows it is snowing. Can't he see it through the window?"

But when she looked herself at the window beside her she was amazed to see that the pane was masked with wet snow and one could scarcely see through it at all. Besides, evening was falling fast.

"I do hope," Teddy remarked, watching his brother start up the aisle, "he tumbles in the right place."

"What is he going to do with that snowball?" demanded Louise.

"I know! I know!" giggled Bobby, in sudden delight. "That man with the silk hander chief over his head is going to get a shower."

"He isn't a man. He's just a fresh kid," declared Ted, but he said it somewhat anxiously now.

"Stop him, somebody!" cried Louise. "He'll get into trouble."

"If you ask me," drawled Bob Henderson, "I think that somebody else is going to get into trouble. I saw that chap stick his foot out and trip Ted before."

Alice B. Emerson

"He did it unknowingly," cried Betty, under her breath. "He's asleep."

"If he is he won't be long," whispered Bobby, clutching at Betty and holding her into the seat. "Let Tommy Tucker be. If that fellow trips him—"

The next instant Tommy did trip. Without any doubt the well shod foot of the man lolling in the seat slid into the aisle as the boy with the snowfall approached, and Tommy pitched over it with almost a certainty of falling headlong. Indeed, he would have gone to the floor of the car had he not let go of the mass of snow in his hands and clutched at the seat arms.

"Whoo!" burst out Teddy Tucker in delight. "Now that fresh kid's got his!"

For the soft snowball in Tommy's hands landed plump upon the handkerchief-covered crown of the person sprawling so ungracefully in the Pullman seat! The victim uttered a howl audible above the drumming of the car wheels. And he leaped upright between the seats of his section, beat the fast-melting snow off his head and face, and displayed the latter to the young peoples' amazement as that of a very stern looking gentleman indeed with a bald head and gray side whiskers.

"Oh, my aunt's cat and all her kittens!" gasped Bob Henderson. "Now Tommy has done it! See who it is, Ted?"

Teddy Tucker was as pale as the snow his brother had brought in from outside and which now showered about the victim of the ill-timed jest.

"Ma—Major Pater! From Salsette! He has an artificial leg, and that's why it was sticking out in the aisle whenever he nodded off. Oh, Jimminy-beeswax! what's going to become of Tommy?"

Alice B. Emerson

CHAPTER X

BEAUTIFUL SNOW

The girls had heard the boys who attended Salsette Academy mention that martinet, Major Pater. Although his infirmity—or injury—precluded his having anything to do with the drilling of the pupils of the academy, in the schoolroom he was the most stern of all the instructors at Salsette.

"Oh, poor Tommy!" gasped Betty, wringing her hands.

"Served him right," declared Louise. "He should not have played that trick. A lame man, too!"

"Oh, Louise!" exclaimed her sister Bobby, "Tommy didn't know it was an artificial limb he was stumbling over."

"And I'm sure I didn't know it was his old peg-leg I tripped on twice," declared Teddy Tucker in high dudgeon. "What did he want to go to sleep for, spraddled all over the aisle?"

He said this in a very low voice, however; and be kept well behind Bob and the girls. As for Timothy Derby and Libbie Littell they actually never heard a word of all this! They sat side by side in one of the sections and read together Spenser's *Faerie Queene*—understanding, it must be confessed, but an infinitesimal part of that poem.

The other passengers near Major Pater, without any doubt, were vastly amused by his condition. The melting snow cascaded off his head and shoulders, and not a little of it went down his neck. Such a military looking and grim-faced man, standing so stiff and upright, seemed all the more ridiculous under these conditions.

"H-r-r-rrp!" barked Major Pater, glaring at Tommy Tucker as though his eyes would burn holes right through that boy's jacket.

Tommy sprang to attention. He was in citizen's dress, as was the major; but Tommy was sure the martinet knew him.

"What do you mean, young man, by pouring a bucket of slush over my head and shoulders?" demanded the angry Major.

"Please, sir, if you'll let me wipe it off—"

Tommy had produced his own handkerchief and made a feeble attempt to attack the melting snow on the Major's shoulders.

"H-r-r-rrp!" barked the Major again, and Tommy translated it as meaning "as you were" and came once more to attention in the middle of the aisle.

One could not really help the angry gentleman, if one was kept standing in that ridiculous position. And the passengers near by were more amused than before by the attitude and appearance of the two engaged in the controversy.

"Are you aware of what you have done?" demanded Major

Alice B. Emerson

Pater, at last "Humph! Tucker of the Fourth, isn't it?"

"Ye—ye—yes, sir," gasped Tommy. Then: "One of the Tuckers, sir."

"Oh! Ah! Can there be two such awkward Tuckers?" demanded Major Paten "Humph! Is this your father, Tucker?"

For by this time Uncle Dick saw what was going on and he approached, smiling it must be confessed, but with a towel secured from the men's lavatory.

"I am acting in the capacity of guardian for the present, sir," said Mr. Gordon frankly. "This is a ridiculous thing; but I do not think the boy quite intended all that happened."

At once he began flicking away the melted snow, and then rubbed Major Pater's bald head dry. All the time he continued to talk to the military academy instructor:

"I grant you that it looks very awkward on Tucker's part. But, you see, Mr.—er—?"

"Ma—Major Pater!" stammered Tommy Tucker.

"Quite so. Major, of course. Major Pater, you will realize that the boy in coming along the aisle—Er, by the way, Tommy, what were you coming for?"

"I was coming to you, Mr. Gordon, to show you how fast the snow was gathering. I—I scraped that ball of it off the step. The porter opened the door for me just a moment. I say, Mr. Gordon, it's a fierce storm!"

Tommy came through this explanation pretty well. Uncle

Dick's understanding smile helped him a good bit.

"Quite so," said Mr. Gordon, and looking at Major Pater again. "Of course, I would never have known it was snowing if you had not undertaken to show me. But you see, Major Pater, your foot was sticking out into the aisle. I saw it. You have the misfortune to—"

"Artificial leg, sir," growled Major Pater.

"Quite so. Well, accidents will happen, you know. There! You are quite dry again. I don't think you will get much sleep here until the porter makes up the berths. Suppose we go into the smoking compartment and soothe our minds, Major?"

"Ah—Humph! Thank you, Mr.—er—?"

"Mr. Gordon," explained Tommy Tucker still standing as though he had swallowed a very stiff poker indeed.

"Ah! Glad to meet you, Mr. Gordon." They shook hands. Then Major Pater shot another command at Tommy: "H-r-r-rrp!" (or so it sounded) and the boy with vast relief dropped his stiff military pose.

The rest of the "live wire octette"—even Timothy and Libbie—were highly delighted by the outcome of Tommy's joke. For, if there is fun in such a practical joke as Tommy had tried to carry through, they thought there was double fun in seeing the biter bitten!

"Now will you be good?" crowed his brother, Ted. "See what you get for being so fresh! Tumbling over his game leg and pitching a wilted snowball at the Major's head. Aren't you ashamed of yourself?"

Alice B. Emerson

"Oh, hush!" grumbled Tommy. "You needn't say anything. He doesn't know which of the Tucker twins it was crowned him with that snowball, and you are just as much in his bad books as I am. Remember that."

"Listen to him!" cried Ted, at once feeling abused. "And Major Pater is near-sighted, too, although he scorns to wear glasses. You've got me into a mess, too, Tommy Tucker."

"There! There!" said Betty Gordon, soothingly. "Never mind. Uncle Dick will smooth him down. But I do think, boys, that you need not have got into trouble at all."

"Huh! that's our natural state," observed Teddy. "Boys out of trouble are like fish out of water. So my dad says. And he ought to know," he grinned. "He has twins."

Tommy considered, however, that he had got out of a bad box pretty easily.

"Your Uncle Dick is fine, Betty," he observed. "Think of his getting on the blind side of Major Pater so easy. But cracky! how that snow did squash all over him," and he ended with a wicked giggle.

"One of your instructors, too!" exclaimed Louise. "For shame!"

"My!" chuckled Bobby, "what we'd like to do to Miss Prettyman at Shadyside!"

"I am afraid Miss Prettyman is no more beloved than Major Pater is."

"Never mind, you girls!" interrupted Tommy, with renewed interest in the storm and trying to peer through the window.

"It's a regular blizzard. When the porter opened the door of the vestibule for me to get that snow, I thought he wouldn't get it shut again."

"Suppose we get stalled?" questioned Louise, inclined to be the most thoughtful of the party.

"Well, suppose we do?" returned Bob. "I tell you we are all right for food, for the dining car—"

"Oh, I forgot to tell you," Tommy put in. "The porter let me into a secret. The diner was dropped about thirty miles back. Broken flange of one wheel and no time, of course, to put on a new wheel."

"Goodness!" exclaimed Betty. "I begin to feel hungry already."

"Of course, we'll pick up another diner?" asked Libbie, though rather doubtfully.

"We'll hope so!" Bobby cried.

"If we get through to Tonawanda, yes," said Tommy Tucker. "That's what the porter told me. But we don't get there, if we are on schedule, until eight o'clock."

"There! I knew I was perishing of hunger," exclaimed Betty. "It's half past four already," she added, looking at her wrist watch.

"Three and a half hours to dinner time?" wailed Bobby. "Oh! That—is—tough!"

"That is, if we make the regular time," Bob said thoughtfully. "And right now, let me tell you, this train is just about

Alice B. Emerson

crawling, and that's all. Humph! The soup sure will get cold in that dining car at Tonawanda, if it waits there to be attached to our train."

"Oh! Oh!" cried Bobby. "Don't let's think of it. I had no idea that snow could be so troublesome."

"Beautiful snow!" murmured Betty. "Say, Libbie. Recite that for us, will you? You know: the poetry about 'Beautiful Snow.' You or Timothy should remember it."

"Pah!" exclaimed Bobby, grumblingly. "I'll give you the proper version:

"Beautiful snow! If it chokes up this train,
It certainly will give me a pain!"

"Goodness me, Bobby!" retorted her cousin, Libbie, "your versifying certainly gives me a pain."

CHAPTER XI

STALLED, AND WITHOUT A DOCTOR

The rapidity with which the storm had increased and the drifts had filled the cuts through which the rails were laid was something that none of the party bound for Mountain Camp had experienced. Unless Uncle Dick be excepted. As Betty said, Mr. Richard Gordon had been almost everywhere and had endured the most surprising experiences. That was something that helped to make him such a splendid guardian.

"Yes," he agreed, when Betty dragged him down the car aisle to the two sections which he had wisely abandoned entirely to his young charges, "we had considerable snow up there in the part of Canada where I have been this fall. Before I came down for the Christmas holidays there was about four feet of snow on the level in the woods and certain sections of the railroad up there had been entirely abandoned for the winter. Horse sleds and dog sleighs do all the transportation until the spring thaw."

"Oh, do you suppose," cried Libbie, big-eyed, "that we may be snowbound at Mountain Camp so that we cannot get back until spring?"

"Not a chance," replied Uncle Dick, laughing heartily. "But

it does look as though we may have to lay by for a night, or perhaps a night and a day, before we can get on to Cliffdale, which is our station."

"In a hotel!" cried Betty. "Won't that be fun?"

"Perhaps not so much fun. Some of these country-town hotels up here in the woods are run in a more haphazard way than a lumber camp. And what you get to eat will come out of a can in all probability."

The boys groaned in unison at this, and even Betty looked woebegone.

"I wish you wouldn't talk about eating, Uncle Dick. Do you suppose we will catch up with that dining car?"

"I do not think we shall. But there is an eating room at the junction we are coming to. We can buy it out. I only hope there will be milk to be had for the little folks. There is at least one baby aboard. It's in the next car."

"But we'll get to this place we're going to by morning, shan't we?" cried Bobby, very much excited.

"We're two hours late already I understand," said Mr. Gordon. "We have little to fear, however I fancy if the storm does not hold up they will not try to push past the junction until morning. We've got to sleep in the car anyway; and if we are on short rations for a few hours it certainly will do you boys and girls little harm. At Cliffdale—"

"Oh, Uncle Dick!" suddenly exclaimed Betty, "that is where Mr. Bolter has sent that beautiful black horse that he bought in England."

"Oh, indeed? I heard of that mare. To Cliffdale? I believe there is a stockfarm there. It is some distance from my friend Canary's camp, however."

"Do you suppose that girl got there?" whispered Bobby to Betty.

"Even if she did, how disappointed she must be," Betty rejoined. "I am awfully sorry for Ida Bellethorne."

"I don't know," said Bobby slowly. "I've been thinking. Suppose she did find your beautiful locket and—and appropriate it for her own use," finished Bobby rather primly.

"You mean steal it," said Betty promptly. "No. I don't think she did. She didn't seem to be that sort of person. Do you know, the more I think of her the more I consider that Mrs. Staples would be capable of doing that."

"Oh, Betty! Finding and keeping your locket?"

Betty nodded with her lips pursed soberly. "I didn't like that woman," she said.

"Neither did I," cried Bobby, easily influenced by her friend's opinion. "I didn't like her a bit."

"But, of course, we don't know a thing about it," sighed Betty. "I do not suppose we should blame either of them, or anybody else. We have no evidence. I guess, Bobby, I am the only one to blame, after all."

"Well, don't mind, Betty dear," Bobby said comfortingly. "I believe the locket will turn up. I told Daddy and he will telephone to the stores once in a while and see if it has been found. And, of course, we have no particular reason to think that you dropped it in Mrs. Staples' shop."

"None at all," admitted Betty more cheerfully. "So I'll stop worrying right now. But I would like to know where Ida Bellethorne is in this blizzard."

"Girl or horse?" chuckled Bobby.

"Girl. I fancy that little cockney hostler, or whatever he is, will look out carefully for the mare. But who is there to care anything about poor Ida?"

Gradually even Betty and Bobby were convinced that there were several other matters to worry about that were connected with neither Ida Bellethorne the girl nor Ida Bellethorne the horse. The belated train finally got to the junction where there was an eating place. But another train had passed, going south, less than an hour before and the lunch counter had been swept almost bare.

Uncle Dick and Major Pater were old travelers, however; and they were first out of the train and bought up most of the food in sight. Others of the passengers purchased sandwiches and coffee and tea to consume at once. Uncle Dick and the military man swept the shelves of canned milk and fruit, prepared cocoa and other similar drinks, as well as all the loaves of bread in sight, a boiled ham complete, and several yards of frankfurters, or, as the Fairfields folks called them, "wienies."

"We know what Mrs. Eustice and Miss Prettyman would say to such provender," said Louise when the party, the boys helping, returned with the spoils of the lunch-room. "How about calories and dietetics, and all that?"

"We may be hungry enough before we see a regular meal in

a dining-car or a hotel to forget all about such things," Uncle Dick said seriously. "There! We are starting already. And we're pushing straight into a blizzard that looks to me as though it would continue all night."

"Well, Uncle Dick," Betty said cheerfully, "we can go to bed and sleep and forget it. It will be all over by morning of course."

Uncle Dick made no rejoinder to this. They had a jolly lunch, getting hot water from the porter for their drink. Bob and the Tucker twins pretty nearly bought out the candy supply on the train, and the girls felt assured that they were completely safe from starvation as long as the caramels and marsh-mallows held out.

By nine o'clock, with the train pushing slowly on, the head locomotive aided by a pusher picked up at the junction, the berths were made up and everybody in the Pullman coach had retired.

Betty, as she lay in her upper berth with Libbie, heard the snow, or sleet, swishing against the side and roof of the car, and the sound lulled her to sleep. She slept like any other healthy girl and knew nothing of the night that passed. The lights were still burning when she awoke. Not a gleam of daylight came through the narrow ground-glass window at her head. And two other things impressed her unfavorably: The train was standing still and not a sound penetrated to the car from without.

Libbie was sound asleep and Betty crept out of the berth without awakening the plump girl. She got into her wrapper and slippers and stole along the aisle to the ladies' room. Nobody as yet seemed to have come from the berths.

Alice B. Emerson

She could not hear the wind or snow when she got into the dressing room. This convinced her at first that the storm was over. But she dropped one of the narrow windows at the top to see out, and found that a wall of hard-pack snow shrouded the window. She tried to break through this drift with her arm wrapped in a towel. But although she stood on a stool and thrust her arm out to her shoulder, her hand did not reach the open air!

"My goodness me!" gasped Betty Gordon. "We're stalled! We're snowbound! What shall we ever do if the snow doesn't melt pretty soon, or they don't come and dig us out?"

She washed in haste, and having brought her clothes with her, she dressed promptly. All the time she was considering what was to be done if, as it seemed, the train could not go on.

Just as she opened the door of the dressing room excited voices sounded at the end of the car. The conductor and the porter were talking loudly. The former suddenly shouted:

"Ladies and gentlemen! is there a doctor in this coach? We want a doctor right away! Day coach ahead! Child taken poison and must have a doctor."

A breathless gabble of voices assured him that there was no physician in the coach. He had already searched the other cars. There was no doctor on the train.

"And we're stalled here in this cut for nobody knows how long!" groaned the conductor. "That woman is crazy in the next car. Her two year old child got hold of some kind of poison and swallowed some of it. The child will die for sure!"

Betty was terribly shocked at this speech. She wriggled past the conductor and the troubled porter, and ran into the car ahead. At first glance she spied the little group of mother and children that was the center of excitement.

Alice B. Emerson

CHAPTER XII

THE TUNNEL

The baby was screaming, the little boy of four or five looked miserably unhappy, and the worn and meager-looking mother was plainly frightened out of her wits. She let the baby scream on the seat beside her while she held the little girl in her lap.

That youngster seemed to be the least disturbed of any of the party. She was a pretty child, and robust. She kicked vigorously against being held almost upside down by her mother (as though by that means the dose of poison could be coaxed out of the child) but she did not cry.

"The little dear!" cooed Betty, pushing through the ring of other passengers. "What has happened to her?"

"She'll be dead in five minutes," croaked a sour visaged woman who bent over the back of the seat to stare at the crying baby without making an effort to relieve the mother in any way.

"What is the poison?" demanded Betty excitedly.

"It—it's—I don't know what the doctor called it," wailed the poor mother. "I had it in my handbag with other drops. Nellie here is always playing with bottles. She will drink out of bottles, much as I can do or say."

Betty was sniffing—that may not be an elegant expression, but it is exactly what she did—and looking all about on the floor.

"Something's been spilled here," she said. "It's a funny odor. Seems to me I remember smelling it before."

"That's the poison," groaned the woman over the back of the seat. "Her ma knocked it out of the young one's hand. Too bad. She's a goner!"

This seemed to Betty very dreadful. She darted an angry glance at the woman. "A regular Mrs. Job's comforter, she is!" thought Betty.

But all the time she was looking about the floor of the car for the bottle. Finally she dropped to her knees and scrambled about among the boots of the passengers. She came up like a diver, with an object held high in one hand.

"Is this it?" she asked.

"That is the bottle, Miss," sobbed the mother. "My poor little Nellie! Isn't there a doctor, anywhere? They say milk is good for some kinds of poison, but I haven't any milk for baby even. That is what makes him cry so. Poor little Nellie!"

Betty had been staring at the label on the bottle. Now she smelled hard at the mouth of it She held the bottle before the woman's eyes.

"Are you sure this is the bottle the child drank out of?"

Alice B. Emerson

she demanded.

"Yes, Miss. That is it. Poor little Nellie!"

"Why! can't you smell?" demanded Betty. "And can't you see? There is no skull and cross-bones on this label. And all that was in the bottle was sweet spirits of niter. I'm sure that won't do your Nellie any lasting harm."

The mother was thunderstruck for a moment—and speechless. The gloomy woman looking over the back of the seat drawled:

"Then it wasn't poison at all?"

"No," said Betty. "And I should think among you, you should have found it out!"

She was quite scornful of the near-by passengers. The mother let the struggling little girl slip out of her lap, fortunately feet first rather than head first, and grabbed up the screaming baby.

"Dear me! You naughty little thing, Nellie! You are always scaring me to death," she said scoldingly. "And if we don't come to some place where I can buy milk pretty soon and get it warmed, this child will burst his lungs crying."

Betty, however, considered that the baby was much too strong and vigorous to be in a starving state as yet. She wondered how the poor women expected to get milk with the train stalled in the snow. She had in her pocket some chocolate wafers and she pacified the two older children with these and then ran back to the sleeping car.

She was in season to head off a procession of excited

Pullman passengers in all stages of undress starting for the day coach with everything in the line of antidote for poison that could be imagined and which they had discovered in their traveling bags.

"Baby's better. She wasn't poisoned at all," Betty told them. "But those children are going to be awfully hungry before long if we have to stay here. Do you know we're snowbound, girls?"

This last she confided to the three Littell girls.

"Won't they dig us out?" asked the practical Louise.

"What a lark!" exclaimed Bobby, clapping her hands.

"Just think! Buried in the snow! How wonderful!" murmured Libbie.

"Cheese!" exclaimed Tommy Tucker, overhearing this. "You'll think it's wonderful. The brakeman told me that the drivers were clogged at six o'clock and the wheels haven't turned since. We're completely buried in snow and it's still snowing. Head engine's an oil-burner and there is plenty of fuel; but there isn't a chance of our being dug out for days."

"How brutal you are," giggled Bobby, who could not be frightened by any misadventure. "How shall we live?"

"After we eat up the bread and ham we will draw lots and eat up each other," Bob observed soberly.

"But those little children can't eat each other," Betty declared with conviction. "Come on Bobby. You're dressed. Let's see what we can do for that poor mother and the babies."

Alice B. Emerson

The two girls had to confer with Uncle Dick first of all. He had charge of the supplies. Betty knew there was some way of mixing condensed milk with water and heating the mixture so that it would do very well at a pinch—the pinch of hunger!—for a nursing child. Uncle Dick supplied the canned milk and some other food for the older children, and Betty and Bobby carried these into the day coach where the little family had spent such an uncomfortable night and were likely to spend a very uncomfortable day as well.

For there was no chance of escaping from their present predicament—all the train crew said so—until plows and shovelers came to dig the train out of the cut.

Of course the conductors and the rest of the crew knew just where they were. Behind them about three miles was a small hamlet at which the train had not been scheduled to stop, and had not stopped. Had the train pulled down there the situation of the crew and passengers would have been much better. They would not have been stalled in this drifted cut.

Cliffdale, to which Uncle Dick and his party were bound, was twenty miles and more ahead. The roadbed was so blocked that it might be several days before the way would be opened to Cliffdale.

"The roads will be opened by the farmers and teams will get through the mountains before the railroad will be dug out," Mr. Gordon told the boys. "If we could get back to that station in the rear we might find conveyances that would take us on to Mountain Camp. If I had a pair of snowshoes I certainly could make it over the hills myself in a short time."

"You go ahead, Mr. Gordon," said Tommy Tucker, "and tell 'em we're coming."

"I'll have to dig out of here and get the webs on my feet first," replied Uncle Dick, laughing.

His speech put an idea in the head of the ingenious Tommy Tucker. While the girls were attending to the children in the car ahead, the twins and Bob and Timothy Derby went through the train to the very end. The observation platform was banked with snow, and the snow was packed pretty hard. But there were some tools at hand and the boys set to work with the two porters and a brakeman to punch a hole through the snowbank to the surface.

It was great sport, although the quartette from Salsette Academy enjoyed it more than the men did. It was fun for the boys and work for the men, and the latter would have given it up in despair if the younger diggers had not been so eagerly interested in the task.

They sloped the tunnel so that it was several yards long before it reached the surface. The snow underneath, they tramped hard; they battered their way through by pressing a good deal of the snow into solid walls on either side. When the roof at the end finally fell in on them, they found that it was still snowing steadily and the wind was pouring great sheets of it into the cut and heaping it yard upon yard over the roofs of the cars. They could barely see the top of the smokestack of the pusher a few feet away.

That locomotive had been abandoned by its crew when the train was stalled. Keeping the boiler of the head engine hot was sufficient to supply the cars with heat and hot water.

"Cricky!" cried Bob. "We've found the way out; but I guess even Uncle Dick wouldn't care to start out in this storm, snowshoes or not. Fellows, we're in a bad fix, just as sure as you live."

Alice B. Emerson

"All right," said Teddy Tucker. "Let's go back and get something to eat before somebody else gets ahead of us. I suppose those girls have given all the milk to those kids up front, and maybe the ham sandwiches too."

"Dear me!" sighed Timothy, "it is like being cast away on a desert island. We are Robinson Crusoes."

"And haven't got even a goat!" chuckled Tommy Tucker.

CHAPTER XIII

AN ALARM

Mr. Richard Gordon was not minded to allow the young folks to portion out the little store of food as they pleased. He and Major Pater, who had now joined the party from Fairfields quite as a matter of course, had considered the use of the supplies to the best advantage. There was not much else to eat on the train, for even the crew had devoured their lunches, and most trainmen when obliged to carry food at all are supplied with huge tin buckets that hold at least three "square meals."

"Though why meals should be 'square' I can't for the life of me see," Betty observed. "Why not 'round' meals? I am sure we manage to get around them when we eat them."

"Quite a philosopheress, aren't you?" joked Bob.

"These rations are not to be considered with philosophy," complained Bobby. "They are too frugal."

In truth, when the bread and meat and crackers and hot drink had been portioned to those needed food most, the amount each received was nothing to gorge upon.

Alice B. Emerson

"If it stops snowing—or as soon as it does," Bob declared, "we've got to get out and make our way back to that station the brakeman says is only three miles away."

"Uncle Dick won't let us try it, I am sure," sighed Betty. "How could we wade through such deep snow?"

"If you had helped dig that tunnel," said Teddy Tucker confidently, "you'd know that the snow is packed so hard you wouldn't sink in very deep in walking."

"But of course, you girls can't go," Tommy said. "We fellows will have to go for supplies."

The girls did not much like this statement. Betty and Bobby at least considered that they were quite as well able to endure the hardships of a tramp through the snow as the boys.

"I'd just like to see that tunnel, and see how hard it is snowing outside," said Betty privately to her chum.

"Let's go look," exclaimed Bobby, equally curious.

Libbie and Timothy had their heads together over a book. Louise and the boys were engaged socially with some of the other passengers in their coach. So Betty and Bobby were able to slip away, with their coats and caps, without being observed.

There were two Pullman coaches and but one day coach besides the express and baggage and mail cars to the train. The passengers in the day coach were confined to that or to the smoker's end of the baggage car ahead. The occupants of the Pullman coaches could roam through both as they pleased; and had the weather been fine it is certain that the young folks from Fairfields would have occupied the observation platform at the rear of the train a good part of the daytime.

They had been shut in by the storm the afternoon before, and now they were doubly shut in by the snow. The doors of the vestibules between the cars could not be opened, for the snow was banked up on both sides to the roofs. That tunnel the boys and train hands had made from the rear platform was the only means of egress for the passengers from the submerged train.

Betty and Bobby passed through the rear car and out upon the snow-banked platform. They saw that several people must have thrust themselves through the tunnel since the boys had made it. Probably these explorers had wished, like the two girls, to discover for themselves just what state the weather was in.

"Dear me!" gasped Bobby, "dare we poke through that hole? What do you think, Betty?"

"The snow is hard packed, just as the boys say. I guess we can risk it," declared the more daring Betty. "Anyway, I can go anywhere Bob Henderson can, my dear. I will not take a back seat for any boy."

"Hear! Hear!" chuckled Bobby. "Isn't that what they cry at political meetings? You have made a good speech, Bettykins. Now go ahead and do it."

"Go ahead and do what?"

"Lead the way through that chimney. My! I believe it has stopped snowing and the boys don't know it."

"Come on then and make sure," Betty cried, and began to

Alice B. Emerson

scramble up the sloping tunnel on hands and knees.

Both girls were warmly dressed, booted, and mittened. A little snow would not hurt them—not even a great deal of snow. And that a great deal had fallen and blown into this railroad cut, Betty and Bobby soon realized when they had scrambled out through what the latter had called "the chimney."

Only a few big flakes drifted in the air, which was keen and biting. But the wind had ceased—at least, it did not blow here in the cut between the hills—and it seemed only an ordinary winter day to the two girls from the other side of the Potomac.

Forward they saw a thin stream of smoke rising into the air from the stack of the front locomotive. The fires in the pusher were banked. It was not an oil-burner, nor was it anywhere near as large a locomotive as the one that pulled the train.

Rearward they could scarcely mark the roadbed, so drifted over was it. Fences and other landmarks were completely buried. The bending telegraph poles, weighted by the pull of snow-laden wires, was all that marked the right of way through the glen.

"What a sight!" gasped Betty. "Oh, Bobby! did you ever see anything so glorious?"

"I never saw so much snow, if that is what you mean," admitted the Virginia girl. "And I am not sure that I really approve of it."

But Bobby laughed. She had to admit it was a great sight. It was now mid-afternoon and all they could see of the sun was a round, hazy ball behind the misty clouds, well down toward the western horizon which they could see through the mouth of this cut, or valley between the hills. At first they beheld not a moving object on the white waste.

"It is almost solemn," pursued Betty, who possessed a keen delight in all manifestations of nature.

"It looks mighty solemn, I admit," agreed Bobby. "Especially when you remember that anything to eat is three miles away and the drifts are nobody knows how many feet deep."

Betty laughed. She was about to say something cheerful in reply when a sudden sound smote upon their ears—a sound that startled the two girls. Somewhere from over the verge of the high bank of the cut on their left hand sounded a long-drawn and perfectly blood-curdling howl!

"For goodness' sake!" gasped Bobby, grabbing her friend by the arm. "What sort of creature is that? Hear it?"

"Of course I hear it," replied Betty, rather sharply. "Do you think I am deaf?"

Only a very deaf person could have missed hearing that mournful howl. It drew nearer.

"Is it a dog?" asked Bobby, almost in a whisper, as for a third time the howl sounded.

"A dog barks, doesn't it? That doesn't sound like a dog, Bobby," said Betty. "I heard one out West. I do believe it is one!"

"One what?" cried Bobby, almost shaking her in alarm and impatience.

Alice B. Emerson

"A wolf. It sounds just like a wolf. Oh, Bobby! suppose there should be a pack of wolves in these hills and that they should attack this train?"

"Wolves!" shrieked Bobby. "*Wolves*! Then me for in-doors! I am not going to stay here and be eaten up by wolves."

As she turned to dive into the tunnel there was a sharper and more eager yelp, and a shaggy animal came to the edge of the bluff to their left and, without stopping an instant, plunged down through the drifts toward the two girls where they stood on the hard-packed snow at the mouth of the tunnel.

"It is a wolf!" wailed Bobby, and immediately disappeared, head first, down the hole in the snow drift.

CHAPTER XIV

THE MOUNTAIN HUT

If Bobby had not gone first and had not stuck half way down the hole with her feet kicking madly just at the mouth of the tunnel, without doubt Betty Gordon would have been driven by her own fears back into the Pullman coach.

That shaggy beast diving from the top of the embankment, plunging, yelping and whining, through the softer drifts of snow, frightened Betty just as much as it had Bobby Littell. The latter had got away with a flying start, however, and her writhing body plugged the only means of escape. So Betty really had to face the approaching terror.

"Oh! Oh!" cried Betty, turning from the approaching beast in despair. "Hurry! Hurry, Bobby Littell! Do you want me to be eaten up?"

But Bobby had somehow cramped herself in the winding passage through the snow, and her voice was muffled as she too cried for help.

However, Bobby's demands for assistance were much more likely to bring it than the cries of the girl outside. The porter heard Bobby first, and when he opened the door of the coach

Alice B. Emerson

several men who were near heard the girl.

"Help! Help! A wolf is eating her!" shrieked the frightened Bobby.

"Ma soul an' body! He must be a-chawin' her legs off!" cried the darkey and he seized Bobby by the wrists, threw himself backward, and the girl came out of the tunnel like an aggravating cork out of a bottle.

"What's this?" demanded Mr. Richard Gordon, who happened to be coming back to the end of the train to look for his niece and her chum.

"Oh, Mr. Gordon!" sputtered Bobby, scrambling up, "it's got her! A wolf! It's got Betty!"

"A wolf?" repeated Uncle Dick. "I didn't know there were any wolves left in this part of the country."

Major Pater was with him. Mr. Gordon grabbed the latter's walking stick and went up that tunnel a good deal quicker than Bobby had come down it. And when he got to the surface he found his niece, laughing and crying at once, and almost smothered by the joyful embraces of a big New-foundland dog!

"A wolf indeed!" cried Mr. Gordon, but beating off the animal good-naturedly. "He must be a friend of yours, Betty."

"Oh, dear me, he did scare us so!" Betty rejoined, getting up out of the drift, trying to brush off her coat, and petting the exuberant dog at the same time. "But it is a dear—and its master must be somewhere about, don't you think, Uncle Dick?"

Its master was, for the next moment he appeared at the top of the bank down which the "wolf" had wallowed. He hailed Uncle Dick and Betty with a great, jovial shout and plunged down the slope himself. He was a young man on snowshoes, and he proved to be a telegraph operator at that station three miles south.

"Wires are so clogged we can't get messages through. But we knew that Number Forty was stalled about here. Going to be a job to dig her out. I've got a message for the conductor," he said when he reached the top of the drift that was heaped over the train.

"Wasn't it a hard task to get here?" Mr. Gordon asked.

"Not so bad. My folks live right over the ridge there, about half a mile away. I just came from the house with the dog. Down, Nero! Behave yourself!"

"We are going to be hungry here pretty soon," suggested Mr. Gordon.

"There will be a pung come up from the station with grub enough before night. Furnished by the company. That is what I have come to see the conductor about."

"I tell you what," said Betty's uncle, who was nothing if not quick in thinking. "My party were bound for Cliffdale."

"That's not very far away. But I doubt if the train gets there this week."

"Bad outlook for us. We are going to Mountain Camp—Mr. Canary's place."

"I know that place," said the telegraph operator. "There is an

Alice B. Emerson

easy road to it from our farm through the hills. Get there quicker than you can by the way of Cliffdale. I believe my father could drive you up there to-morrow."

"In a sleigh?" cried Betty delightedly. "What fun!"

"In a pung. With four of our horses. They'd break the road all right. Ought to start right early in the morning, though."

"Do you suppose you could get us over to your house to-night?" asked Mr. Gordon quickly. "There are a good many of us—"

"How many in the party?" asked the young man. "My name's Jaroth—Fred Jaroth."

Mr. Gordon handed him his card and said:

"There are four girls, four boys, and myself. Quite a party."

"That is all right, Mr. Gordon," said Fred Jaroth cheerfully. "We often put up thirty people in the summer. We've a great ranch of a house. And I can help you up the bank yonder and beat you a path through the woods to the main road. Nothing simpler. Your trunks will get to Cliffdale sometime and you can carry your hand baggage."

"Not many trunks, thank goodness," replied Mr. Gordon. "What do you think, Betty? Does it sound good?"

"Heavenly!" declared his niece.

Just then a brakeman came up through the tunnel to find out if the wolf had eaten both the gentleman and his niece, and the telegraph operator went down, feet first, to find the conductor and deliver his message.

"Then the idea of going on to Mountain Camp by sledge suits you, does it, young lady?" asked Mr. Gordon of Betty.

"They will all be delighted. You know they will, Uncle. What sport!"

The suggestion of the telegraph operator did seem quite inspired. Mr. Gordon and Betty reentered the train to impart the decision to the others, and, as Betty had claimed, her young friends were both excited and delighted by the prospect.

In half an hour the party was off, Betty and her friends bundled up and carrying their bags while Mr. Gordon followed and Fred Jaroth led the way on his snowshoes and carrying two suitcases. He said they helped balance him and made the track through the snow firmer. As for Nero, he cavorted like a wild dog, and that, Bobby said, proved he was a wolf!

Once at the top of the bank they found it rather easy following Jaroth through the woods. And when they reached the road—or the place where the highway would have been if the snow had not drifted over fences and all—they met the party from the station bringing up food and other comforts for the snowbound passengers. As the snow had really stopped falling it was expected that the plow would be along sometime the next day and then the train would be pulled back to the junction.

"But if this man has a roomy sled and good horses we shall not be cheated out of our visit to Mountain Camp," Mr. Gordon said cheerfully.

The old farmhouse when they reached it certainly looked big enough to accommodate them all. There was a wing thrown out on either side; but those wings were for use only in the summer. There were beds enough and to spare in the main part of the house.

When they sat down to Mrs. Jaroth's supper table Bob declared that quite evidently famine had not reached this retired spot. The platters were heaped with fried ham and fried eggs and sausages and other staple articles. These and the hot biscuit disappeared like snow before a hot sun in April.

Altogether it was a joyous evening that they spent at the Jaroth house. Yet as Betty and Bobby cuddled up together in the bed which they shared, Betty expressed a certain fear which had been bothering her for some time.

"I wonder where she is, Bobby?" Betty said thoughtfully.

"Where who is?" demanded her chum sleepily.

"That girl. Ida Bellethorne. If she came up here on a wild goose chase after her aunt, and found only a horse, what will become of her?"

"I haven't the least idea," confessed Bobby.

"Did she return before this blizzard set in, or is she still up here in the woods? And what will become of her?"

"Gracious!" exclaimed the sleepy Bobby, "let's go to sleep and think about Ida Bellethorne to-morrow."

"And I wonder if it is possible that she can know anything about my locket," was another murmured question of Betty's. But Bobby had gone fast asleep then and did not answer.

Under the radiance of the big oil lamp hanging above the kitchen table, the table itself covered with an old-fashioned red and white checked cloth, the young folks bound for Mountain Camp ate breakfast. And such a breakfast!

Buckwheat cakes, each as big as the plate itself with "oodles of butter and real maple syrup," to quote Bob.

"We don't even get as good as this at Salsette," said Tommy Tucker grimly. "Oh, cracky!"

"I want to know!" gibed his twin, borrowing a phrase he had heard New England Libbie use on one occasion. "If Major Pater could see us now!"

Libbie and Timothy forgot to quote poetry. The fact was, as Bobby pointed out, buckwheat cakes like those were poems in themselves.

"And when one's mouth is full of such poems, mere printed verses lack value."

Romantic as she was, Libbie admitted the truth of her cousin's remark.

A chime of bells at the door hastened the completion of the meal. The boys might have sat there longer and, like boa-constrictors, gorged themselves into lethargy.

However, adventure was ahead and the sound of the sledge bells excited the young people. They got on their coats and caps and furs and mittens and trooped out to the "pung," as the elder Jaroth called the low, deep, straw-filled sledge to which he had attached four strong farm horses.

There were no seats. It would be much more comfortable

Alice B. Emerson

sitting in the straw, and much warmer. For although the storm had entirely passed the cold was intense. It nipped every exposed feature, and their breath hung like hoar-frost before them when they laughed and talked.

During the night something had been done to break out the road. Mr. Jaroth's horses managed to trample the drifts into something like a hubbly path for the broad sled-runners to slip oven They went on, almost always mounting a grade, for four hours before they came to a human habitation.

The driver pointed his whipstock to a black speck before them and higher up the hill which was sharply defined against the background of pure white.

"Bill Kedders' hut," he said to Mr. Gordon. "'Tain't likely he's there this time o' year. Usually he and his wife go to Cliffdale to spend the winter with their married daughter."

"Just the same," cried Bob suddenly, "there's smoke coming out of that chimney. Don't you see it, Uncle Dick?"

"The boy's right!" ejaculated Jaroth, with sudden anxiety. "It can't be that Bill and his woman were caught by this blizzard. He's as knowing about weather signs as an old bear, Bill is. And you can bet every bear in these woods is holed up till spring."

He even urged the plodding horses to a faster pace. The hut, buried in the snow to a point far above its eaves, was built against a steep hillside at the edge of the wood, with the drifted road passing directly before its door. When the pung drew up before it and the horses stopped with a sudden shower of tinkling bell-notes, Mr. Jaroth shouted:

"Hey, Bill! Hey, Bill Kedders!"

There was no direct reply to this hail. But as they listened for a reply there was not one of the party that did not distinguish quite clearly the sound of weeping from inside the mountain hut.

Alice B. Emerson

CHAPTER XV

THE LOST GIRL

"That ain't Bill!" exclaimed Jaroth. "That's as sure as you're a foot high. Nor yet it ain't his wife. If either one of them has cried since they were put into short clothes I miss my guess. Huh!"

He hesitated, standing in the snow half way between the pung and the snow-smothered door of the hut. Sheltered as it had been by the hill and by the woods, the hut was not masked so much by the drifted snow on its front. They could see the upper part of the door-casing.

"By gravy!" ejaculated Mr. Jaroth, "it don't sound human. I can't make it out. Funny things they say happen up here in these woods. I wouldn't be a mite surprised if that crying— or—"

He hesitated while the boys and girls, and even Mr. Gordon, stared amazedly at him.

"Who do you think it is?" asked Uncle Dick finally.

"Well, it ain't Bill," grumbled Jaroth.

The sobbing continued. So engaged was the person weeping in the sorrow that convulsed him, or her, that the jingling of the bells as the horses shook their heads or the voices of those in the pung did not attract attention.

Jaroth stood in the snow and neither advanced nor retreated. It really did seem as though he was afraid to approach nearer to the hut on the mountain-side!

"That is a girl or a woman in there," Bob declared.

"Huh!" exclaimed Bobby sharply. "It might be a boy. Boys cry sometimes."

"Really?" said Timothy. "But you never read of crying boys except in humorous verses. They are not supposed to cry."

"Well," said Betty, suddenly hopping out of the sleigh, "we'll never find out whether it is a girl or a boy if we wait for Mr. Jaroth, it seems."

She started for the door of the hut. Bob hopped out after her in a hurry. And he took with him the snow-shovel Jaroth had brought along to use in clearing the drifts away if they chanced to get stuck.

"You'd better look out," said Jaroth, still standing undecided in the snow.

"For what?" asked Bob, hurrying to get before Betty.

"That crying don't sound natural. Might he a ha'nt. Can't tell."

"Fancy!" whispered Betty in glee. "A great big man like him afraid of a ghost—and there isn't such a thing!"

Alice B. Emerson

"Don't need to be if he is afraid of it," returned Bob in the same low tone. "You can be afraid of any fancy if you want to. It doesn't need to exist. I guess most fears are of things that don't really exist Come on, now. Let me shovel this drift away."

He set to work vigorously on the snow heap before the door. Mr. Gordon, seeing that everything possible was being done, let the young people go ahead without interference. In two minutes they could see the frozen latch-string that was hanging out. Whoever was in the hut had not taken the precaution to pull in the leather thong.

"Go ahead, Betty," said Bob finally. "You push open the door. I'll stand here ready to beat 'em down with the shovel if they start after you."

"Guess you think it isn't a girl, then," chuckled Betty, as she pulled the string and heard the bar inside click as it was drawn out of the slot.

With the shovel Bob pushed the door inward. The cabin would have been quite dark had it not been for a little fire crackling on the hearth. Over this a figure stooped—huddled, it seemed, for warmth. The room was almost bare.

"Why, you poor thing!" Betty cried, running into the hut. "Are you here all alone?"

She had seen instantly that it was a girl. And evidently the stranger was in much misery. But at Betty's cry she started up from the hearth and whirled about in both fear and surprise.

Her hair was disarranged, and there was a great deal of it. Her face was swollen with weeping, and she was all but blinded by her tears. At Betty's sympathetic tone and words she burst out crying again. Betty gathered her right into her arms—or, as much of her as she could enfold, for the other girl was bigger than Betty in every way.

"You?" gasped the crying girl. "How—how did you come up here? And in all this snow? Oh, this is a wilderness—a wilderness! How do people ever live here, even in the summer? It is dreadful—dreadful! And I thought I should freeze."

"Ida Bellethorne!" gasped Betty. "Who would ever have expected to find you here?"

"I know I haven't any more business here than I have in the moon," said the English girl. "I—I wish I'd never left Mrs. Staples."

"Mrs. Staples told us you had come up this way," Betty said.

Immediately the other girl jerked away from her, threw back her damp hair, and stared, startled, at Betty.

"Then you—you found out? You know—"

"My poor girl!" interrupted Betty, quite misunderstanding Ida's look, "I know all about your coming up here to find your aunt. And that was foolish, for the notice you saw in the paper was about Mr. Bolter's black mare."

"Mr. Bolter's mare?" repeated Ida.

"Now, tell me!" urged the excited Betty. "Didn't you come to Cliffdale to look for your aunt?"

"Yes. That I did. But she isn't up here at all."

By this time Uncle Dick and the others were gathered about the door of the hut. Jaroth, with a glance now and then at his horses, had even stepped inside.

"By gravy!" ejaculated the man, "this here's a pretty to-do. What you been doing to Bill Kedders' chattels, girl?"

"I—I burned them. I had to, to keep warm," answered Ida Bellethorne haltingly. "I burned the table and the chairs and the boxes and then pulled down the berths and burned them. If you hadn't come I don't know what I should have done for a fire."

"By gravy! Burned down the shack itself to keep you warm, I reckon!" chuckled Jaroth. "Well, we'd better take this girl along with us, hadn't we, Mr. Gordon? She'll set fire to the timber next, if we don't, after she's used up the shack."

"We most surely will take her along to Mountain Camp," declared Betty's uncle. "But what puzzles me, is how she ever got here to this, lonely place."

"I was trying to find the Candace Farm," choked Ida Bellethorne.

"I want to know!" said Jaroth. "That's the stockfarm where they pasture so many sportin' hosses. Candace, he makes a good thing out of it. But it's eight miles from here and not in the direction we're going, Mr. Gordon."

"We will take her along to Mountain Camp," said Uncle Dick. "One more will not scare Mrs. Canary, I am sure."

Ida brought a good-sized suitcase out of the hut with her. She had evidently tried to walk from Cliffdale to the stockfarm, carrying that weight. The girls were buzzing over the appearance of the stranger and the boys stared.

"Oh, Betty!" whispered Bobby Littell, "is she Ida Bellethorne?"

"One of them," rejoined Betty promptly.

"Then do you suppose she has your locket?" ventured Bobby.

To tell the truth, Betty had not once thought of that!

CHAPTER XVI

THE CAMP ON THE OVERLOOK

Mountain Camp was rightly named, for it was built on the side of one mountain and was facing another. Between the two eminences was a lake at least five miles long and almost as broad. The wind had blown so hard during the blizzard that the snow had not piled upon the ice at all, although it was heaped man-high along the edges. The pool of blue ice stretched away from before Mountain Camp like a huge sheet of plate glass.

The two storied, rambling house, built of rough logs on the outside, stood on a plateau called the Overlook forty feet above the surface of the lake. Indeed the spot did overlook the whole high valley.

The hills sloped down from this height in easy descents to the plains. Woods masked every topographical contour of the surrounding country. Such woods as Betty Gordon and her friends had never seen before.

"Virginia forests are not like this," confessed Louise Littell. "The pines are never so tall and there is not so much hardwood. Dear me! see that dead pine across the lake. It almost seems to touch the sky, it is so tall."

This talk took place the next morning when they had all rested and, like all healthy young things, were eager for adventure. They had been welcomed by Mr. and Mrs. Canary in a way that put the most bashful at ease.

Even Ida Bellethorne had soon recovered from that sense of strangeness that had at first overpowered her. The girls had been able to help her out a little in the matter of dress. She appeared at the dinner table quite as one of themselves. Betty would not hear of Ida's withdrawing from the general company, and for a particular reason.

In truth, Betty felt a little condemned. She had considered a suspicion of Ida's honesty, and afterward she knew it could not be so! The English girl had no appearance of a dishonest person. Betty saw that Uncle Dick was favorably disposed toward Ida. If he did not consider her all right he surely would not have introduced her to Mr. and Mrs. Canary as one of his party.

Nor did Uncle Dick allow Ida to tell her story the evening they arrived at the camp on the Overlook. "To-morrow will do for that," he had said.

At breakfast time there were so many plans for exciting adventure discussed that Betty surely would have forgotten all about Ida Bellethorne's expected explanation had it not been for the lost locket. The possibility that Ida knew something about it had so impressed Betty that nothing else held her interest for long.

Every one had brought skates from Fairfields, and the great expanse of blue ice—no ice is so blue as that of a mountain lake—was unmarked. Naturally skating was the very first pleasure that beckoned.

"Oh, I'm just crazy to get on skates!" cried Bobby.

"I think I'll be glad to do some skating myself," came from Libbie, who had been reading a book even before breakfast.

"What do you say to a race on skates?" came from Tommy Tucker.

"I think we had better get used to skating up here before we talk about a race," said Bob. "This ice looks tremendously hard and slippery. You won't be able to do much on your skates unless they are extra sharp."

"Oh, I had 'em sharpened."

"Don't forget to wrap up well," admonished Mrs. Canary. "Sometimes it gets pretty cold and windy."

"Not to say anything about its being cold already," answered Bobby. "My, but the wind goes right through a person up here!"

While the other seven ran off for skates and wraps, Betty nodded to Uncle Dick and then, tucking her arm through that of Ida Bellethorne, urged her to follow Mr. Gordon from the breakfast room to a little study, or "den," that was possibly Mr. Canary's own.

"Now, girls," said Uncle Dick in his quiet, pleasant way and smiling with equal kindness upon his niece and the English girl, "let us get comfortable and open our hearts to each other. I think you know, Ida, that Betty and I are immensely interested in your story and we are hungry for the details. But not altogether out of mere curiosity. We hope to give you aid in some way to make your situation better. Understand?"

"Oh, Mr. Gordon, I quite understand that," said the English girl seriously and without smiling. "I never saw such friendly people as you are. And you both strangers to me! If I were at home I couldn't find better friends, I am sure."

"That's fine!" declared Uncle Dick. "It is exactly the way I want you to feel. Betty and I are interested. Now suppose you sit down and tell us all about it."

"Where shall I begin?" murmured the girl thoughtfully, hesitating.

"If I were you," returned Uncle Dick, with a smile, "I would begin at the beginning."

"Oh, but that's so very far back!"

"Never mind that. One of the most foolish mistakes which I see in educational methods is to give the children lessons in modern history without any reference to ancient history which comes to them in higher grades. Ancient history should be gone into first. Suppose, Ida, you begin with ancient history."

"Before Ida Bellethorne was born, do you mean?" asked the English girl doubtfully.

"Which Ida Bellethorne do you mean?" asked Mr. Gordon, while Betty stared.

"I was thinking of my beautiful black mare. The darling! She is seven years old now, Mr. Gordon; but I think that in those seven years enough has happened to me to make me feel three times seven years old."

"Go ahead, Ida," said the gentleman cheerfully. "Tell it in

Alice B. Emerson

your own way."

Thus encouraged, the girl began, and she did tell it in her own way. But it was not a brief way, and both Mr. Gordon and Betty asked questions and that, too, increased the difficulty of Ida's telling her story.

She had been the only living child of Gwynne Bellethorne, who had been a horse breeder and sometimes a turfman in one of the lower English counties. She had been motherless since her third birthday. Her only living relative was her father's sister, likewise Ida Bellethorne, who had been estranged from her brother for several years and had made her own way on the continent and later in America on the concert stage.

Ida, the present Ida, remembered seeing her aunt but once. She had come to Bellethorne Park the very week the black mare was foaled. When they all went out to see the little, awkward, kicking colt in the big box stall, separated from its whinnying mother by a strong barred fence, the owner of the stables had laughingly named the filly after his sister.

"But," Ida told them, "father told Aunt Ida that the filly was to be my property. He had, I think, suffered many losses even then. He made a bill of sale, or something, making the filly over to me; but I was a minor, and after father died my guardian had that bill of sale. He showed it to me once. I don't see how Mr. Bolter could have bought my lovely mare when I got none of the money for her."

This was not, however, sticking to the main thread of the story. Ida knew that although her aunt had come to the Park in amity, there was a quarrel between her father and aunt before the haughty and beautiful concert singer went away, never more to appear at Bellethorne, not even to attend her brother's funeral.

Before that sad happening the mare, Ida Bellethorne, had come to full growth and as a three-year-old had made an astonishing record on the English race tracks. The year Mr. Bellethorne died he had planned to ship her to France for the Grand Prix. Her name was in the mouths of every sportsman in England and her fame had spread to the United States.

The death of her father had signaled the breaking up of her home and the severing of all home ties for Ida. Like many men of his class, Mr. Bellethorne had had no close friends. At least, no honorable friends. The man he had chosen as the administrator of his wrecked estate and the guardian of his unfortunate daughter, Ida felt sure had been dishonorable.

There seemed nothing left for Ida when the estate was "settled." One day Ida Bellethorne, the mare, had disappeared, and Ida the girl could learn nothing about her or what had been done with her. At that she had run away from her guardian, had made her way to Liverpool, had taken service with an American family sailing for the United States, and so had reached New York.

"I found a letter addressed to Aunt Ida after my father died," explained the girl, choking back a sob. "On the envelope in pencil father had written to me to find Aunt Ida and give it to her. He hoped she would forgive him and take some interest in me. I've got that letter safe in here." She touched the belt that held her blouse down so snugly. "I hope I'll find Aunt Ida and be able to give her the letter. I remember her as a most beautiful, tall woman. I loved her on sight. But, I don't know—"

"Cheer up!" exclaimed Mr. Gordon, beamingly. "We'll find her. I take it upon myself to say that Betty and I will find her

Alice B. Emerson

for you. Sha'n't we, Betty?"

"Indeed we will. If she is singing in this country of course it will be comparatively easy to find her."

"Do you think so?" asked Ida Bellethorne doubtfully. "I have not found it so, and I have been searching for her for three months now. This is such a big country! I never imagined it so big until I began to look for Aunt Ida. It seems like looking for a needle in a haystack."

CHAPTER XVII

OFF ON SNOWSHOES

Mr. Gordon encouraged the English girl at this point in her story by assuring her that he would, before returning to Canada, put the matter in the hands of his lawyers and have the search for the elder Ida Bellethorne conducted in a more businesslike way.

"How did you expect to find your aunt," he asked, "when you first landed in New York?"

"I knew of a musical journal published there which I believed kept track of people who sang. I went to that office. The last they knew of my aunt she was booked to sing at a concert in Washington," Ida said sadly. "The date was the very day I called at the office. I hurried to buy a ticket to Washington. But the distance was so great that when my train got into Washington the concert was over and I could do nothing more until the next day."

"And then?" asked Uncle Dick.

"She had gone again. All the company had gone and I could find nobody who knew anything about her. I—I didn't have much money left," confessed the girl. "And things do cost so

Alice B. Emerson

much here in your country. I was frightened. I walked about to find a cheap lodging and reached that street in Georgetown where Mrs. Staples has her shop."

"I see," commented Uncle Dick.

"So I asked Mrs. Staples. She was English too, and she offered me lodgings and a chance to serve in her shop. I took it. What else could I do?"

"You are a plucky girl, I must say. Don't you think so. Betty?" said Uncle Dick.

"I think she is quite wonderful!" cried his niece. "And think of her making those blouses so beautifully! You know, Ida, Bobby bought the blue one of Mrs. Staples."

"I am glad, if you like them," said the other girl, blushing faintly. "I had hard work to persuade Mrs. Staples to pay for that one on the chance of your coming back for it."

"Well," interposed Uncle Dick, "tell us the rest. You thought you heard of your Aunt Ida up here, in the mountains?"

"Yes, Mr. Gordon," said Ida. "I read it in the paper. But the notice must have referred to my dear little mare. I never dreamed she had been sent over here. I never dreamed of it!"

"No?"

"Of course I didn't! And when I got to Cliffdale there was nobody who had ever heard of my aunt. There are two hotels. One of them is closed at this time of year. At the other there was no such guest."

"Dear me! How disappointed you must have felt," murmured Betty.

"You can't imagine! But in talking with the clerk at the hotel I got news of my little darling."

"Meaning the mare, of course?" suggested Uncle Dick.

"Yes. She had arrived the night before and had been taken directly to Candace Farm. The clerk told me how to get there. I did not feel that I could afford to hire anybody to take me there. And I knew nobody. So I set out to walk day before yesterday morning."

"Before it began to snow?" asked Betty.

"Yes, Miss Gordon."

"Oh, please," cried Betty, "call me Betty. I'm not old enough to be Miss Gordon. To a girl, anyway," she added. "With a strange boy it would be different."

The English girl consented, and then went on with her story.

"It was cloudy but I did not know anything about such storms as you have here. Oh, dear me, how it snowed and blew! I got to that little house and I could open the door. If I had had to go many yards farther I would have fallen down and been covered by the snow."

"You poor dear!" murmured Betty, putting an arm around the other girl.

Ida gave her a tearful smile, and Betty kissed her. And then the latter suddenly remembered again her lost locket. She gave a little jump in her chair. But she did not speak of it.

Not for a moment did she believe Ida Bellethorne would be guilty of stealing her trinket. Uncle Dick evidently did not think of that possibility, either. Could Betty suggest such a matter when already Ida was in so much trouble? At least, she would wait and see what came of it. So she hugged Ida more closely and said:

"Go on. What else?"

"Not much else, Betty," said the English girl, wiping her eyes again and smiling. "I just stayed there in that house until you came along and saved me. There was nothing to burn but the furniture in the house, and I burned it. I suppose the poor man who owns it will want to be paid. Oh, dear!"

"I wouldn't worry about that," said Mr. Gordon, cheerfully. "You seem to have come through a good deal. I'd take it easy now. Mrs. Canary and the girls are glad to have you here. When we go back to town we will take you with us and see what can be done."

"Thank you, Mr. Gordon. You are very kind. I should like to know about my little mare. She is a darling! How this Mr. Bolter came to get her—"

"Oh, Ida!" cried Betty, breaking in suddenly, "do you know a little man, a crooked little man, named Hunchie Slattery?"

"My goodness, Betty! Of course I remember Hunchie. He worked in our stables."

"He is with Ida Bellethorne, your pretty mare. He takes care of her. I talked with him at Mr. Bolter's farm in Virginia. The mare has a cough, and she was sent up here to get well. And I heard Mr. Bolter himself tell Hunchie Slattery that he was to go with her."

"Dear me, Betty! if I could find Hunchie, too, I'd feel better. He might be able to tell me how it came that my mare was taken away and sold. She really did belong to me, Mr. Gordon. Mr. Jackwood, father's administrator and my guardian, showed me the bill of sale making me Ida's owner. And even if I was a minor, wouldn't that be a legal transfer paper?"

"I am not sure of the English law, my dear. But it seems to me it would be in this country. At any rate, that will be another thing to consult my lawyers about. I understand Bolter paid somewhere near twenty thousand dollars for the mare. It would be quite a fortune for you, Ida."

"Indeed it would. And the mare is worth all of four thousand pounds, I know. Father always said there was no better mare in all England than Ida Bellethorne, and Aunt Ida might be proud to have such a horse named after her."

"We are not far from the Candace Farm and perhaps we can get over there before we leave Mountain Camp," Mr. Gordon said kindly. "Then you can see your horse and the man from home. I will get a statement from this jockey, or hostler, or whatever he is, and it may aid my lawyers in their search for the facts regarding the sale of the mare to Mr. Bolter."

"Thank you very kindly, Mr. Gordon."

The conference broke up and Betty ran out to join her mates on the lake. Ida could not skate. And, anyway, she preferred to sit indoors with Mrs. Canary. Ida had the silk for another sweater in her bag, and that very hour she began to knit an over-blouse for Libbie, who had expressed a desire to possess one like those Betty and Bobby had bought.

The skating was fine, but the wind had risen again and this

Alice B. Emerson

time it was a warm wind. The snow grew soft on the surface, and when the party came up the bluff for luncheon it was not easy to walk and they sank deeply into the snow.

"This is a weather breeder," said Mr. Canary, standing on the porch to greet them. "I fear you young folks have come to Mountain Camp at the beginning of the roughest part of the winter."

"Don't apologize for your weather, Jack," laughed Uncle Dick. "If it grows too boisterous or unpleasant outside, these young people must find their fun indoors."

And this is what they did for the next two days. The temperature moderated a good deal, and then it rained. Not a hard downpour, but a drifting "Scotch mist" that settled the snowdrifts and finally left them saturated with water.

Then back came the frost—sharp, snappy and robust. The air cleared like magic. The sun shone out of a perfectly clear sky. Just to put one's head out of the door make the blood tingle.

Meanwhile both the girls and boys had found plenty of interesting things to do indoors, as Uncle Dick had prophesied. Especially the boys. Under the teaching of Uncle Dick and Mr. Canary they had learned to string snowshoes. Mr. Canary had the frames and the thongs of which the webs are woven. Even Timothy neglected the library to engage in this fascinating work.

Of course, the girls must have webs as well. Betty and Bobby were particularly eager to learn to walk on snowshoes and, as Bob Henderson said, they "pestered" the boys until sufficient pairs of webs were made to enable the entire party to try walking on them when the time was ripe.

On the third morning, just at dawn, there was a heavy snow squall for an hour. It left about four inches of downy snow upon the hard-packed and slippery surface of the drifts.

"This is an ideal condition," said Mr. Gordon with enthusiasm. "My feet itch to be off on the webs myself. After breakfast we will try them out. Now remember the rules I have been telling you, and see how well you can all learn to shuffle over this snow."

Thoughtful Bob had strung an extra pair of shoes for Ida. He knew that Betty did not want the English girl left out of their good times. And all the crowd liked Ida. Although she was in the main a very quiet girl, as one grew to know her she proved to possess charming qualities both of mind and heart.

Ida was not as warmly dressed for venturing into the open as the other girls. But Mrs. Canary, one of the kindest souls in the world, mended this defect. She furnished Ida with a fur coat and gloves that secured her from frostbite.

The whole party turned out gaily. Having been confined to the house for almost forty-eight hours, they were as full of life as colts. But in a few minutes the nine of them were on snowshoes and watched and instructed by Uncle Dick were learning their first lesson in the rather ticklish art of scuffling over the soft snow without tripping and plunging headlong into it.

Not that there were not many laughable accidents. The capers both boys and girls involuntarily cut led to shouts of laughter, and sometimes to a little pain. For the frozen crust underneath the light surface snow offered a rather hard foundation when one fell flat.

The necessary falls incident to learning the right trick of

Alice B. Emerson

handling one's self on snowshoes soon cured the first enthusiasm of several of the party. Louise, for instance, found it too strenuous for her liking. And Timothy got a bump on the back of his head that no phrenologist could have easily described.

The second day, however, Betty, Bobby and Ida, with Bob and Tommy Tucker, were just as enthusiastic on the subject of snowshoeing as at first. While the others swept off a part of the lake just below the Outlook, the snowshoeing party set off on their first real hike through the woods; and that hike led to an unexpected adventure.

CHAPTER XVIII

GREAT EXCITEMENT

Mr. Richard Gordon was, as Betty and Bob often declared, the very best uncle that ever lived! One good thing about him they thought was that he never "fussed."

"He isn't always wondering what you are going to do next and telling you not to," explained Bob to Ida Bellethorne as the party started out from Mountain Camp. "Not like a woman, oh, no!"

"Hush, bad boy!" cried Bobby. "What do you mean, throwing slurs at women?"

"You know even if Mrs. Canary had seen us start off she would have given us a dozen orders before we got out of earshot. And she's a mighty nice woman, too. Almost as nice as your mother, Bobby," finished Bob.

"Bob doesn't like chaperons," giggled Betty.

"Nor me," said Tommy Tucker, sticking close to Bobby Littell as he always did when Roberta would let him. "Uncle Dick suits me as a chaperon every time."

Alice B. Emerson

Uncle Dick had let the party troop away on their snowshoes without advising them when to return or asking where they were going, and presently Betty and Bob formed a sudden plan about their hike.

From one of the men working about the camp Bob had got directions regarding the nearest way to Candace Farm. Ida longed to go there. It was but seven miles away in a direct line, and now, when Betty spoke of going there, Bob said that, with the aid of his compass, he knew he could find it without difficulty.

"We didn't mention it to Uncle Dick, but he won't be bothered about it," said Bob. "We've got all day. We can tell him where we have been when we get back, which will be just the same."

"Will it, Bob?" the girl asked doubtfully. "But of course there is nothing really wrong in going."

"I—should—say—not!" exploded Bob. "I'm sure it will be all right with Uncle Dick, Betty. Remember how he let us roam and explore in Oklahoma?"

The others in the party were not troubled by doubts in the least. They went hurrying through the snow with shouts and laughter; and if any forest animals were astir that day they must have been frightened by the noise the party made scrambling along on snowshoes. Not one of them but fell at times—and the very "twistiest" kind of falls! But nobody was hurt; although at one point Bobby fell flat on her back at the verge of a steep descent and there was no stopping her until she plunged into a deep drift at the bottom.

Tommy kicked off his snowshoes and ran down to haul her out while the others, seeing that she was unhurt, shouted their glee. Bobby was not often in a fix that she could not get out of by her own exertions. Being such an energetic and independent girl, she would not often accept help of her boy friends, especially of Tommy who hovered around her like a moth around a candle.

But when she had lost her snowshoes she found the soft snow so much deeper than she expected at the bottom of that hill that she was glad indeed to accept Tommy's aid. He dragged her out of the drift and set her upright. Even then she found that she could not climb up again by herself to where her friends were enjoying her discomfiture.

"Come on!" cried Tommy, who had kicked his own snow-shoes off at the top of the slide. "Give us your hand, Bobby. We'll make it somehow."

But they did not "make it" easily. It seemed as though they could climb only so high and then slide back again. Under the shallow top snow the frozen crust was like pebbled glass. Tommy could barely kick the toes of his boots into it to make steps, and just as he had secured a footing in a particularly slippery place, Bobby would utter a shriek and slide to the bottom again.

Even Betty was almost ill with laughter as this occurred over and over again. But the Tucker twin finally proved himself to be master of the situation. He was determined to get Bobby to the top of the hill, and he succeeded.

Tom Tucker was a strong lad. Stooping, he commanded the girl to put her arms over his shoulders so that he could seize both wrists with one hand. Then he bent forward, carrying Bobby on his back and her weight upon his aided in breaking through the snow-crust and getting a footing.

Alice B. Emerson

He plodded up the slope, a little at a time, and after a while Betty and Bob helped them to the level brink of the hill. Tommy fell to the snow panting, and Bobby was inclined to scold for a minute. Then she gave Tommy one of her rare smiles and helped him up. She was not often so kind to him.

"You are a good child, Tommy Tucker," she proclaimed saucily, as she beat the loose snow off his coat. "In time you may be quite nice."

Betty and Ida Bellethorne praised him too; but Bob continued to laugh and when the party started on again the others learned why he was so amused.

The way to Candace Farm lay right down that slope to the bottom of which Bobby had tumbled, and all the exertion Tommy had put forth to save her was unnecessary. Bob led them along a lane right past the spot where Tommy had pulled the girl out of the snowbank!

"That's the meanest trick that was ever played on me!" declared Bobby, in high wrath at first. Then she began to appreciate the joke and laughed with the others. "I was going to tell the folks at home how Tommy saved me from the peril of being buried in the snowbank; but I guess I'd better not," she observed. "Don't blame me, Tommy. Give it to Bob."

"Ill get square with Bob," grumbled the Tucker twin. "No fear of that."

Bobby remained kind to him however; and as Tommy frankly admired her he was repaid for his effort. But every time Bob looked at Tom he burst out laughing.

They had struck into a straight trough in the snow, with

maples on either side standing gaunt and strong, and a windrow of drifted snow where the fences were supposed to be—a road which Bob said the man at Mountain Camp had told him led straight to Candace Farm.

"Wish we had brought a sled with us," Tommy said. "We could have ridden the girls on it. Aren't you tired, Bobby?"

"Not as tired as you are, I warrant," she said, laughing at him. "Poor Tommy!"

"Aw, you go fish! I could carry you a mile and not feel it. Gee! What's this coming?"

Far down the snow-covered road they first heard shouts, then a cloud of snow-dust spurted into the air and hid whatever it was coming along the way toward them. Bob immediately drew Betty and Ida to one side of the road and Tommy urged Bobby to follow.

Suddenly out of the cloud of flying snow appeared a horse's head and plunging fore feet. Then another and another! They came along the road at a plunging, blundering pace, snorting and neighing. Behind them were men, evidently trying to stop the runaways.

"Colts!" shouted Bob. "Yearlings. All young horses. And just about wild. Remember that bunch we saw in Oklahoma, Betty, that was being driven to the shipping station? They are wild as bears."

Ida Bellethorne did not seem to be much disturbed by the possibility of the horses doing them any harm. She stood out before her companions and stared at the coming herd eagerly. The black mare she loved so, however, was not in this bunch of runaways.

The young stock swept past the watching party from Mountain Camp, their pace rapid in spite of the hard going. They kept to the snow-covered road, however. Behind them came half a dozen men, wind-spent already and not a little angry.

"Why didn't you stop 'em?" bawled one red-faced fellow. "If they spread out in some open pasture we'll be all day gathering them."

"Easy to stop 'em, I guess," returned Tommy. "They'd have trampled us down."

"Could stop a snowslide easier, I guess," Bob suggested. "But I tell you: We'll give you a hand collecting them. How did they get away?"

"Went over the paddock fence like a flock of sheep. Snow is so deep, you know," said the red-faced man. "Come on, you boys, if you will. The girls can go on to the house and Mrs. Candace will let 'em warm up. It's only a little way."

The "little way" proved to be a good two miles; but the three girls did not falter. They saw the big farmhouse and the great barns and snow-filled paddocks a long way ahead.

"I'll be glad of that 'warm'," confessed Betty, as they turned in at the entrance to the lane. "And maybe Mrs. Candace will give us a cup of tea."

At that moment Bobby clutched her arm and pointed up the lane. "See there! He'll fall! Oh, look!"

Betty was as startled as her chum when she spied what Bobby had first seen. A little, crooked man was crawling out above the hay door of the main barn upon a timber that was here thrust out from the framework and to which was attached a block and fall. The rope had evidently fouled in the block and he was trying to detach it.

"That's Hunchie Slattery!" gasped Betty, "What a chance he is taking!"

For everything was sheathed in ice from the effect of the rain and frost of the night before. That timber was as slippery as glass.

Ida Bellethorne set off on a run for the barn; but unlike Bobby she did not say a word. Had she thought of any way to help the crooked little man, however, she was too late. Hunchie suddenly slipped, clutched vainly at the rope, which gave under his weight, and he came down "on the run."

The rope undoubtedly broke his fall. He would have been killed had he plunged immediately to the frozen ground beneath.

As it was, when the three girls reached him, he was unconscious and it was plain by the attitude in which he lay that his leg was broken.

Alice B. Emerson

CHAPTER XIX

THE EMERGENCY

"Poor Hunchie!" murmured Ida Bellethorne, "I hope it wasn't because he was surprised to see me that he fell."

"His surprise did not make that timber slippery with ice," said Betty, looking up. "Oh! Here's a lady!"

A comfortable looking woman with a shawl over her head was hurrying from the kitchen door of the Candace farmhouse.

"What has happened to that poor man? He's been battered and kicked about so much, it would seem, there ain't much can happen to him that he hasn't already suffered.

"Ah! Poor fellow!" she added, stooping over the senseless Hunchie. "What a deal of trouble some folks seem bound to have. And not another man on the place!"

She stood up again and stared at the three girls. Her broad, florid face was all creased with trouble now, but Betty thought she must ordinarily be a very cheerful woman indeed.

"They've gone chasing the young stock that broke away. Dear me! what is going to happen to this poor fellow? Bill and the rest may be gone for hours, and there's bones broke here, that's sure."

"Where's a doctor?" asked Bobby eagerly.

"Eleven miles away, my dear, if he's an inch. Dr. Pevy is the only man for a broken bone in these woods. Poor Hunchie!"

"Can't we get him into his bed?" asked Betty. "He'll freeze here."

"You're right," replied the woman, who afterward told them she was Mrs. Candace. "Yes, we'll take him into the house and put him into a good bed. Can you girls lift him?"

They could and did. And without too much effort the three transported the injured man, who was but a light weight, across the yard, into the house, and to a room which Mrs. Candace showed them. He began to groan and mutter before they managed to get him on the bed.

There was an old woman who helped Mrs. Candace in the house, and the two removed Hunchie's outer garments and made him as comfortable as possible while the girls waited in much excitement in the sitting room.

"He saw one of you girls and knows you," said Mrs. Candace, coming out of the bedroom. "But he talks about that mare, Ida Bellethorne."

"This is Ida Bellethorne," said Betty, pointing to the English girl.

"I declare! I thought Hunchie was out of his head. How

Alice B. Emerson

comes you are named after that horse, girl?"

Ida explained her connection with the black mare and with Hunchie.

"You'd better go in and talk to him. Maybe it will ease his pain. But that shin bone is sticking right through the flesh of his leg. It's awful! And he's in terrible pain. If Bill don't come back soon—"

"Isn't there any man on the place?" asked Betty, interrupting.

"None but them with Bill hunting the young stock."

"And the boys—our friends—have gone with them," explained Betty. "Somebody must get the surgeon."

"How are we going to do it? The telephone wires are down," explained Mrs. Candace. "And there ain't a horse properly shod for traveling on this ice. I fear some of that young stock will break their legs."

"We saw them skating all over the road," said Bobby. "But how gay and excited they were!"

"A ridin' horse would have to go at a foot pace," explained Mrs. Candace, "unless it was sharpened. I don't know—"

Ida had gone into the bedroom to speak with the injured man. She looked out at this juncture and excitedly beckoned to Betty. Betty ran in to find the crooked little man looking even more crooked and pitiful than ever under the blankets. He was groaning and the perspiration stood on his forehead. That he was in exceeding pain there could be no doubt.

"He says Ida Bellethorne is sharpened," gasped Ida.

"Oh! You mean she is fixed to travel on ice on frozen ground?"

"I 'ad to lead 'er up 'ere from the station, Miss. Ain't I saw you before, Miss?" said Hunchie, staring at Betty. "At Mr. Bolter's?"

"Yes, yes!" cried Betty. "Can the mare travel on this hard snow?"

"Yes, ma'am. I didn't draw the calks for I exercised 'er each d'y, I did. I didn't want 'er to fall. An' now I failed myself!"

The two girls looked at each other significantly. Ida was easily led out of the room. Betty put the question to her.

"That's just it, Betty," said the English girl, almost in tears. "I never learned to ride. I never did ride. My nurse was afraid to let me learn when I was little, and although I love horses, I only know how to drive them. It's like a sailor never having learned to swim."

Betty beat her hands together in excitement. "Never mind! Never mind!" she cried. "I can ride. I can ride any horse. I am not afraid of your Ida Bellethorne. And none of the boys or men is here. I'll go for the doctor."

"I don't know if it is best for you to," groaned Ida.

"Call Mrs. Candace." They were in the kitchen, and Ida ran to summon the farm woman while Betty got into her coat. Mrs. Candace came, hurrying.

"What is this I hear?" she demanded. "I couldn't let you ride that horse. You will be thrown or something."

Alice B. Emerson

"No I shan't, Mrs. Candace. I can ride. And Hunchie says the mare is sharpened."

"So she is. I had forgotten," the woman admitted thoughtfully.

"And the poor fellow suffers so. Some lasting harm may be done if we don't get a surgeon quickly. Where does Dr. Pevy live?" demanded Betty urgently.

The fact that the injured hostler was really in great pain and possibly in some danger, caused Mrs. Candace finally to agree to the girl's demand. Betty ran out with Ida to get the mare and saddle her. Betty was not dressed properly for such a venture as this; but she wore warm undergarments, and stout shoes.

The black mare was so gentle with all her spirit and fire that Betty did not feel any fear. She and Ida led the beautiful creature out upon the barn floor and found saddle and bridle for her. In ten minutes Betty was astride the mare and Ida led her out of the stable.

Mrs. Candace had already given Betty clear directions regarding the way to Dr. Pevy's; but she now stood on the door-stone and called repetitions of these directions after her.

Bobby waved her fur piece and shouted encouragement too. But Ida Bellethorne ran into the house to attend the injured Hunchie and did not watch Betty and the black mare out of sight as the others did.

CHAPTER XX

BETTY'S RIDE

When Betty Gordon and her young friends had set out from Mountain Camp on their snowshoe hike the sun shone brilliantly and every ice-covered branch and fence-rail sparkled as though bedewed with diamond dust. Now that it was drawing toward noon the sky was overcast again and the wind, had Betty stopped to listen to it, might be heard mourning in the tops of the pines.

But Ida Bellethorne, the black mare, gave Betty no opportunity of stopping to listen to the wind mourn. No, indeed! The girl had all she could do for the first mile or two to keep her saddle and cling to the reins.

When first they set forth from the Candace stables the mare went gingerly enough for a few rods. She seemed to know that the frozen crust of the old drifts just beneath the loose snow was perilous.

But her sharpened calks gave her a grip on the frozen snow that the wise mare quickly understood. She lengthened her stride. She gathered speed. And once getting her usual swift gait, with expanded nostrils and erect ears, she skimmed over the frozen way as a swallow skims the air. Betty had never

Alice B. Emerson

traveled so fast in her life except in a speeding automobile.

She could easily believe that Ida Bellethorne had broken most of the track records of the English turf. She might make track history here in the United States, if nothing happened to her!

Betty was wise enough to know that, had Mr. Candace been at home, even in this earnest need for a surgeon he would never have allowed the beautiful and valuable mare to have been used in this way. But there was no other horse on the place that could be trusted to travel at any gait.

Ida Bellethorne certainly was traveling! The speed, the keen rush of the wind past her, the need for haste and her own personal peril, all served to give Betty a veritable thrill.

If Ida made a misstep—if she went down in a heap—Betty was pretty sure that she, herself, would be hurt. She retained a tight grip upon the reins. The mare was no velvet-mouthed animal. Betty doubted if she had the strength in her arms to pull the creature down to a walk now that she was started.

The instructions Mrs. Candace had given the girl pointed to a descent into the valley for some miles, and almost by a direct road, and then around a sharp turn and up the grade by a branch road to the village where Dr. Pevy lived. Betty was sure she would not lose her way; the question was, could she cling to the saddle and keep the mare on her feet until the first exuberance of Ida's spirit was controlled? The condition of the road did not so much matter, for once the mare found that she did not slip on the crust she trod the way firmly and with perfect confidence.

"She is a dear—she undoubtedly is," Betty thought. "But I feel just as though I were being run away with by a steam engine and did not know how to close the throttle or reverse the engine. Dear me!"

She might well say "dear me." Uncle Dick would surely have been much worried for her safety if he could know what she was doing. Betty by no means appreciated in full her danger.

Indeed, she scarcely thought of danger. Ida Bellethorne seemed as sure-footed as a chamois. Her calks threw bits of ice-crust behind her, and she never slipped nor slid. There was nobody on the road. There was not even the mark of a sledge, although along the ditch were the shuffling prints of snowshoes. Some pedestrian had gone this way in the early morning.

This was not the road by which Betty and her friends had been transported by Mr. Jaroth. There was not even a hut like Bill Kedders' beside it. In places the thick woods verged right on the track on either side and in these tunnels it seemed to be already dusk.

It flashed into Betty's mind that there might be savage animals in these thick woods. Bears, and wild cats, and perhaps even the larger Canadian lynx, might be hovering in the dark wood. It would not be pleasant to have one of those animals spring out at one, perhaps from an overhanging limb, as the little mare and her rider dashed beneath!

"Just the same," the girl thought, "at the pace Ida Bellethorne is carrying me, such wild animals couldn't jump quick enough to catch me. Guess I needn't be afraid of them."

There were perils in her path—most unexpected perils. Betty would never have even dreamed of what really threatened her. For fifteen minutes Ida Bellethorne galloped on and the girl knew she must have come a third of the way to Dr.

Pevy's office.

The mare's first exuberance passed. Of her own volition she drew down to a canter. Her speed still seemed almost phenominal to the girl riding her, but Betty began to feel more secure in the saddle.

They reached the top of a steep hill. The hedge of tall pines and underbrush drew closer in on either side. The road was very narrow. As the mare started down the incline it seemed as though they were going into a long and steep chute.

Before this Betty had noted the ice-hung telephone and telegraph wires strung beside the road. Sheeted in the frozen rain and snow the heavy wires had dragged many of the poles askew. Here and there a wire was broken.

It never entered the girl's mind that there was danger in those wires. And, perhaps, in most of them there was not. But across this ravine into which the road plunged, and slantingly, were strung much heavier wires—feed cables from the Cliffdale power station over the hill.

"Why, look at those icicles!" exclaimed Betty, with big eyes and watching the hanging wires ahead. "If they fell they would kill a person, I do believe!"

She tugged with all her might at Ida Bellethorne's reins, and now, well breathed, the mare responded to the unuttered command. She came into a walk. Betty continued to stare at the heavily laden wires spanning the road, the heavier power wires above the sagging series of telephone and telegraph wires.

In watching them so closely the girl discovered another, and even more startling fact. One of the poles bearing up the feed wires was actually pitched at such an angle from the top of the bank on the right hand that Betty felt sure the wires themselves were all that held the pole from falling.

"There is going to be an accident here," declared the girl aloud. "I wonder the company doesn't send out men to fix it. Although I guess they could not prop up that pole. It has gone too far."

Even as she spoke the mare stopped, snorting. Her instinct was more keen than Betty's reasoning.

With a screeching breaking and tearing of wood and wire the trembling pole fell! Betty might, had she urged her mount, have cleared the place and escaped. But the girl lacked that wisdom.

The pole fell across the deep road and its two heavy cables came in contact with the wires strung from the other poles below. Instantly the ravine was lit by a blinding flash of blue flame—a flame that ran from wire to wire, from pole to pole, melting the ice that clung to them, hissing and crackling and giving off shooting spears of flame that threatened any passer-by.

The mare, snorting and fearful, scrambled back, swerved, and tried to escape from the ravine; but Betty had her under good control now. She had no spurs, but she yanked savagely at the bit and wheeled Ida Bellethorne again to face the sputtering electric flames that barred the road.

Only a third of the way to the doctor's and the way made impassable! What should she do? If she turned back, Betty did not know where or how to strike into the thick and pathless forest. Hunchie, suffering from his injured leg, must be aided as soon as possible. Her advance must not be stayed.

Yet there before her the sparking, darting flames spread the width of the ravine. Burning a black hole already in the deep drifts, the crossed wires forbade the girl to advance another yard!

CHAPTER XXI

BETTY COMES THROUGH

Betty admitted that she was badly frightened. She was afraid of the crossed wires, and would have been in any case. The spurting blue flames she knew would savagely burn her and Ida Bellethorne if they touched them, and the wires might give a shock that would kill either girl or horse.

But seven miles or so beyond those sputtering flames was Dr. Pevy's office. And Dr. Pevy was needed right away at Candace Farm.

A picture of poor Hunchie lying white and moaning in the bed rose in Betty's memory. She could not return and report that it was impossible for her to reach the doctor's office. Afraid as she was of the crossed wires, she was more afraid of showing the white feather.

If Bob Henderson were here in her situation Betty was sure he would not back down. And if Bob could overcome difficulties, why couldn't Betty? The thought inspired the girl to do as Bob would do—come through.

"I must do it!" Betty choked, holding the mare firmly headed toward the writhing, crackling wires. "Ida! Get up! You can jump it. You—just—must!"

The black mare crouched and snorted. Betty would have given a good deal for tiny spurs in the heels of her shoes or for a whip to lay along the mare's flank. Spirited as the creature was, and well trained, too, her fear of fire made her shrink from the leap.

There was a width of six feet of darting flames. The electricity in the heavy cables was melting the other wires, and from the broken end of each wire the blue light spurted. The snow was melting all about, turning black and yellow in streaks. Betty did not know how long this would keep up; but every minute she delayed poor Hunchie paid for in continued suffering.

"We must do it!" she shrieked to the horse. "You've got to—there!"

She whipped off her velvet hat and struck Ida Bellethorne again and again. The mare crouched, measured the distance, and leaped into the air. Well for her and for Betty that Ida Bellethorne had a good pedigree; had come of a long line of forebears that had been taught to jump hedges, fences, water-holes and bogs. None of them had ever made such a perilous leap as this!

The mare landed in softening snow, for the scathing flames were melting the drifts on either side. Betty had felt the rush of heat rising from the cables and had put her hat over her face.

Ida Bellethorne squealed. Without doubt she had been scorched somewhere. And now secure on her feet she darted away through the ravine, running faster than she had run while Betty had bestrode her.

Betty could not glance back at the sputtering wires. She must keep her gaze fixed ahead. Although at the speed the mare was now running it is quite doubtful if the girl could have retarded her mount in any degree. They came to the forks that Mrs. Candace had told her of, and Betty managed to turn the frightened mare up the steeper road to the left. There were few landmarks that the snow had not hidden; but the way to Dr. Pevy's was so direct that one could scarcely mistake it.

Ida Bellethorne began to cool down after a while and Betty could guide her more easily. She had begun to talk to the pretty creature soothingly, and leaned forward in her saddle to pat the mare's neck.

"I don't blame you for being scared, Ida Bellethorne," crooned Betty. "I was scared myself, and I'm scared yet. But don't mind. Just be easy. Your pretty black apron in front is all spattered with froth, poor dear! I wonder if this run has done your cough any harm—or any good. Anyway, you haven't coughed since we started."

But Betty knew that if the mare stood for a minute she must be covered and rubbed down. She had this in her mind when she came to the blacksmith shop and the store, directly opposite each other. Dr. Pevy's, she had been told, was the second house beyond on the blacksmith side of the road.

It proved to be a comfortable looking cottage with a barn at the back, and she urged Ida Bellethorne around to the barn without stopping at the house. The barn door was open and a man in greasy overalls was tinkering about a small motor-car. He was a pleasant-looking man with a beard and eyeglasses and Betty was sure he must be the doctor before he even spoke to her.

"Hullo!" exclaimed the amateur machanic, rising up with a wrench in one hand and an oil can in the other. "Whew! That mare has been traveling some. And such a beauty! You're from Bill Candace's I'm sure. Did she run away with you? Here, let me help you."

But Betty was out of the saddle and had led the mare in upon the floor, although Ida Bellethorne looked somewhat askance at the partly dismantled car.

"Needn't be afraid of the road-bug, my beauty," said Dr. Pevy, putting out a knowing hand to stroke the mare's neck. "She must be rubbed down and a cloth put on her—"

"I know," said Betty hastily. "I'll do it if you'll let me. But can you go back with me, Doctor?"

"To the Candace Farm?"

"Yes, sir. A man has been seriously hurt and there was nobody else to come."

"Wonder you got here without having a fall," said Dr. Pevy.

"She is sharpened. And she is a dear!" gasped Betty. "But I hope you can start right away. Hunchie is suffering so."

"Can't use the road-bug, that's sure," said Dr. Pevy, glancing again at the car. "That's why I was doctoring her now while the snow is too deep. But I still have old Standby and the sleigh. I'll start back with you in a few minutes and we'll lead the mare. The exercise will do her good. My! What a handsome creature she is."

"Yes, sir. She is quite wonderful," said Betty; and while they gave Ida Bellethorne the attention she needed Betty told the doctor all about Hunchie and her ride through the forest. When Dr. Pevy heard about the broken wires in the road, he went to the house and telephoned to the Cliffdale power house to tell them where the break was. The linemen were already searching for it.

"That peril will be averted immediately," he said coming back with his overalls removed, a coat over his arm and carrying his case in his other hand. "That's it, my dear. Walk her up and down. Such a beauty!"

He got out his light sleigh and then led Standby, a big, red-roan horse, out on the floor to harness him.

"These automobiles are all right when the snow doesn't fly," Dr. Pevy remarked. "But up here in the hills we have so much snow that one has to keep a horse anyway or else give up business during the winter. You were a plucky girl to come so far on that mare, my dear. A Washington girl, you say?"

"We just came from Washington," Betty explained. "But I can't really claim to belong there. I—I'm sort of homeless, I guess. I do just love these mountains and this air."

"This air," commented Dr. Pevy, "smells just now of a storm. And I think it may drizzle again. Now, if you are ready, my dear."

He unbuckled Ida Bellethorne's bridle rein and made it a leading rein. He helped Betty into the sleigh and gave her the rein to hold. The mare led easily, and merely snorted when Standby leaned into the collar and started the sleigh.

The roan was heavy footed, and his shoes, too, were calked. They started off from the village at a good jog with the

Alice B. Emerson

blanketed black mare trotting easily behind the sleigh.

Betty tried to mould her velvet hat into shape. It had been a hat that she very much prized, and was copied after one Ada Nansen wore, and Ada set the fashions at Shadyside. But that little hat would never be the same again after being used as a goad for Ida Bellethorne. Betty sighed, and gave up her attempt.

When they came to the place in the ravine where the wires were down Dr. Pevy drew up Standby. The mare snorted, recognizing the spot. But the electrical display was over, for the power had been turned off.

"You certainly must have had a narrow squeak here," remarked the physician, as he looked at the fallen wires.

"Oh, Doctor, it was awful!" breathed Betty. "I thought sure that we were going to have the worst kind of accident."

"The company ought really to put up a new line of poles, so many of these are getting rotten," was the doctor's reply. "But I suppose they are hard up for money these days, and can afford only the necessary repairs."

The sleigh climbed the mountain after that to the Candace Farm. As they came in sight of it Betty saw the troop of young stock being driven in through the lane, and saw Bob and Tommy with the stock farmer and his men. It was well she had ventured for the doctor on the black mare, or poor Hunchie Slattery would have suffered much longer without medical attention.

Bobby ran out to meet them when the sleigh came into the yard. Mrs. Candace stood at the back door explaining to the red-faced man, her husband. It was Bob who came to take the leading rein of the black mare from Betty's hand.

"Cricky!" he exclaimed. "What have you been up to now, Betsey? Is this that English mare? Isn't she a beauty! And you've been riding her?"

"I've been flying on her," sighed Betty, "Don't talk, Bob! I never expect to travel so fast in the saddle again unless I become a jockey. And I know I am growing too fat for that."

CHAPTER XXII

ON THE BRINK OF DISCOVERY

The three girls and their boy friends remained at the farm until Dr. Pevy had set the bad fracture that Hunchie had suffered and the poor little man had been made as comfortable as he could be made at the time. He had been badly shaken in falling so far at the barn, and the surgeon declared he would be confined to his bed for some weeks.

"And oo's to take care of Ida Bellethorne, I ask you?" demanded Hunchie faintly. "Mr. Bolter hexpects me to give hundivided hattention to 'er."

"She shall have the best of care," said Candace, the farmer, warmly. "A mare like her ought to be bedded down in roses. The way she took this little girl over the drifts was a caution. She is some horse, she is! We will give her the best of attention, Hunchie, never you fear."

The cockney was so much troubled about his charge that he seemed to have forgotten Ida Bellethorne, the girl. But Betty heard him say one thing to Ida before they left.

"You ought to be 'appy, Miss Ida, even if the mare was sold. She brought a good price, and ev'rybody about Bellethorne

Park knows as Mr. Bellethorne give 'er to you when she was a filly. I 'ope you'll come to see us again—me and the mare."

"I surely will, Hunchie," said the English girl.

But when they came out of the house and bade the family good-bye, Betty saw that Ida was very grave. Hunchie's words seemed to have been significant.

It was late in the afternoon when the quintette arrived at Mountain Camp. Mrs. Canary had expressed some anxiety about them, but Uncle Dick had scouted any peril that might threaten the young folks. He admitted that he had overlooked some possibilities when he heard the full account of their adventures—and especially of his niece's adventures—at the dinner table.

"I declare, Betty," he said with some little exasperation, "I believe if you were locked inside a trunk with only gimlet holes to breathe through you would manage to get into trouble."

"I think I'd be in trouble fast enough in that case," answered Betty, laughing.

"I don't know," said Louise thoughtfully. "Locked up in a box, you really couldn't get into much harm, Betty."

"Sure she could get into trouble," declared Bobby. "Bees could crawl in through the gimlet holes and sting her."

"I'd like to have seen her jumping that fire on horseback," sighed Libbie. "It must have been wonderful!"

Mr. Gordon looked rather disturbed as he stared at his niece.

Alice B. Emerson

"That's exactly what I shouldn't want to see her do," he said. "I do not know what I am going to do if, as she gets older, she grows more energetic," he added to Mr. and Mrs. Canary. "Betty is more than a handful for a poor bachelor uncle, I do believe!"

He forbade any more excursions away from the camp after that unless the excursionists took some adult person with them. He went himself to Candace Farm to see Hunchie Slattery; but he took only Ida Bellethorne with him. They went on their snowshoes. During this trip Mr. Gordon won the abiding confidence of the girl.

Meanwhile the youthful visitors at Mountain Camp allowed no hour to be idle. There was always something to do, and what one could not think of in the way of fun another could.

Mr. Canary's men had smoothed a coasting course down the hillside to the lake not a quarter of a mile from the Overlook. There was a nest of toboggans in one of the outhouses. Tobogganing afforded the nine young people much sport.

For the others insisted that Ida Bellethorne share in all their good times. She declared she never would get Libbie's blouse done in time; but Libbie said that she could finish it afterward and send it on to Shadyside. Just now the main thing was to crowd as much fun as possible into the remaining days of their vacation.

The young folks from Fairfields were paired off very nicely; but they did not let Ida feel that she was a "fifth wheel," and she really had a good time. These snow-sports were so unfamiliar to her that she enjoyed them the more keenly.

"I do think these boys are so nice," she said to Betty as they climbed the hill from the lakeshore, dragging the toboggan behind them by its rope.

"Of course they're nice," said the loyal Betty. "Especially Bob Henderson. He's just like a brother to me. If he wasn't nice to you I should scold him—that I should, Ida."

"I never can repay you for your kindness," sighed the English girl, quite serious of visage. "And your uncle, too."

Betty flashed her a penetrating look and was on the verge of speaking of something that she, at least, considered of much importance. Then she hesitated. Ida had never mentioned the possibility of Betty's having dropped anything in Mrs. Staples' store. Betty shut her lips tight again and waited. If Ida did know anything about her lost locket, Betty wanted the English girl to speak of it first.

They went in to dress for dinner that afternoon just before a change in the weather. A storm had been threatening for some hours, and flakes of snow began to drift down before they left the slide.

"Let's dress up in our best, girls," Louise said gaily. "Put on our best bibs and tuckers. Make it a gala occasion. Teddy, be sure and scrub behind your ears, naughty boy!"

"I feel as though I ought to be in rompers the way you talk," said the Tucker twin, but he laughed.

The boys ran off to "primp," and what the girls did to make themselves lovely, Libbie said "was a caution!" One after the other they came into Betty's and Bobby's room and pirouetted to show their finery. Ida had been decked out very nicely by her friends, and her outfit did not seem shabby in the least.

Alice B. Emerson

But the English girl noted one thing about Betty, and it puzzled her. The other girls from Shadyside School wore their pieces of jewelry while Betty displayed not a single trinket. As the other girls were hurrying out to join the boys and descend to the big hall, Ida held Betty back.

"Where is it, Betty?" she asked. "Don't you wear it at all? Are you afraid of losing it again?"

"What do you mean?" asked Betty, her heart pounding suddenly and her eyes growing brighter. Ida Bellethorne placed her hand upon Betty's chest, looking at her closely as she asked the question:

"Didn't Mrs. Staples give it to you? That beautiful locket, you know. Aren't you allowed to wear it?"

CHAPTER XXIII

CAN IT BE DONE?

"Dear me!" exclaimed Betty. "How curious you are. I am not allowed to wear my diamond earrings that Doctor and Mrs. Guerin gave me, of course. They are the old-fashioned kind for pierced ears, and would have to be reset, and diamonds are too old for me anyway. But Uncle Dick lets me wear any thing else I own—"

"That locket," questioned Ida. "That pretty locket. It did fall out of your bag in the shop, didn't it, Betty?"

"My goodness!" stammered Betty, "did you find it?"

"I picked it up," said Ida soberly. "Mrs. Staples would not let me run after you with it. But she promised to give it to you when you came and asked for it."

"She did? She never—"

Then Betty hesitated a moment. She remembered clearly just what had been said in the little neighborhood shop when she and Bobby had called there to get Bobby's blue over-blouse.

"It's a fact, I never asked her for it," she said slowly. "No, I

Alice B. Emerson

never. I just asked her if she had found anything, and she said 'No.'"

"She would! That would be like her!" cried Ida Bellethorne. "She is a person who prides herself upon being exactly honest; and I guess that means barely honest. Oh, Betty Gordon!"

"Well, now what's the matter?" asked Betty.

"Did—did you know you lost it in Mrs. Staples' shop?"

"No. I didn't know where I lost it. I only thought—"

"That I might have picked it up and said nothing about it?" demanded Ida Bellethorne.

"Why Ida! I would not have hurt your feelings by saying anything about it for the world," said Betty honestly. "That was why I didn't tell you. You see, if you really had known nothing about the locket when I asked you, all the time you would be afraid that I suspected you. Isn't that so?"

"You dear, good girl!" gasped Ida, dabbling her eyes with her handkerchief. "And I didn't say anything because I thought you would think I wanted a reward for returning it."

"So, you see, I couldn't speak of it. But now, of course, we'll get it away from Mrs. Staples. I think she's horrid mean!"

Betty expressed her opinion of the shopwoman vigorously, but she put her arms around the English girl at the same time and kissed her warmly.

"You're a dear!" repeated Ida.

"You're another!" cried Betty gaily. "Now come on! Maybe those boys will eat up all the dinner, and I am so hungry!"

One of the men arrived from Cliffdale during dinner with the mail and the information that another cold rain was falling and freezing to everything it touched.

"The whole country about here will be one glare of ice in the morning," said Mr. Canary. "You young folks will have all the sledding you care for, I fancy. I have seen the time when, after one of these ice storms, one might coast from here to Midway Junction on the railroad, and that's a matter of twenty miles."

"What a lark that would be," cried Tommy Tucker. "Some slide, eh, Bob?"

"How about walking back?" asked the other boy promptly, grinning.

Letters and papers were distributed. There was at least one letter for everybody but Ida, and Betty squeezed her hand under the table in a comforting way.

When they all retired from the table and gathered in groups in the big living room where the log fire roared Uncle Dick beckoned Betty to him. He put a letter from Mrs. Eustice into the girl's hand and at one glance she "knew the worst."

"Oh Betty!" gasped Louise, "what's the matter?"

For Betty had emitted a squeal of despair. She shook the paper before their eyes.

"Come on, Betty!" cried Bob. "Get it out—if it's a fishbone."

Alice B. Emerson

"It's all over!" wailed Betty. "Measles don't last as long as we thought they did. Shadyside opens two days from to-morrow, and we have got to be there. That's Monday. Oh, dear, dear, dear!"

"Say a couple more for me, Betty," growled Teddy Tucker. "I suppose Salsette will open too. Back to Major Pater and others too murderous to mention."

"And the Major's got it in for you Tucker twins," Bob reminded him wickedly.

"That's Tom's fault," grumbled Teddy. "If he hadn't sprung that snowball stunt—Oh, well! What's the use?"

"Life, Ted believes," said Louise, "is just one misfortune after another. But I do hate to leave here just as we have got nicely settled. My goodness! what's the matter with Ida? Something's happened to her, too."

Ida had sprung to her feet with one of the recently arrived New York papers in her hand. Actually she was pale, and it was no wonder the company stared at her when her cheeks were usually so ruddy.

"What is the matter, dear?" asked Mrs. Canary.

Betty went to the English girl at once and put an arm about her shoulders.

"Did you see something in the paper that frightened you, Ida?" she asked.

"It doesn't frighten me," replied the girl, with trembling lips. "See. Read it. This time I am sure it is my aunt. See!"

Uncle Dick joined the group about the excited girl. Her color had come back into her cheeks now and her eyes shone. She was usually so self-contained and quiet that Mr. Gordon now thought perhaps they had not really appreciated how much the hope of joining her aunt meant to Ida.

"Read it aloud, Betty," said her uncle quietly.

"Oh! Here's her name! It must be right this time!" cried Betty; and then she obeyed her uncle's request:

"'The Toscanelli Opera Company, Salvatore Toscanelli manager, which has made a very favorable impression among the music lovers of the East and Middle West during the last few months, will sail for Rio Janeiro on Sunday on the *San Salvador* of the Blue Star Line. The company has been augmented by the engagement of several soloists, among them Madam Ida Bellethorne, the English soprano, who has made many friends here during the past few years.'"

"Day after to-morrow!" exclaimed Bobby, the first to speak. "Why! maybe if you can go to New York you will see her, Ida."

"Day after to-morrow," repeated Ida, anxiously. "Can I get to New York by that time? I—I have a little money—"

"Don't worry about the money, honey," Betty broke in. "You will have to start early in the morning, won't she, Uncle Dick?"

"If she is to reach the steamer in time, yes," said the gentleman rather doubtfully.

"Oh! if I don't get there what shall I do?" cried Ida. "Rio

Alice B. Emerson

Janeiro, why, that is in South America! It would cost hundreds of your dollars to pay my passage there. I must get to Aunt Ida before she sails. I must!"

"Now, now!" put in Mrs. Canary soothingly. "Don't worry about it, child. That will not help. We will get you to the train to-morrow—"

"If we can," interrupted her husband softly.

He beckoned Uncle Dick away and they went out through the hall to look at the weather, leaving the young folks and Mrs. Canary to encourage the English girl.

Outside the two men did not find much in the appearance of the weather to encourage them. It was raining softly, for there was no wind; and it was freezing as fast as it fell.

"And that old shack-a-bones I keep here during the winter isn't sharpened. Ought to be, I know. But he isn't," grumbled Jonathan Canary.

"No use to think of snowshoes if it freezes, Jack," rejoined Mr. Gordon. "It is too far to the railroad anyway. I doubt if these children get to school on time."

"Telephone wires are down again. I just tried to get Cliffdale before dinner. This is a wilderness up here, Dick."

"I am sorry for that young English girl," mused Mr. Gordon. "She is fairly eaten up with the idea of getting in touch with her aunt. Good reason, too. She has told me all about it. She carries a letter from her dead father to the woman and he begged the girl to be sure to put it into his sister's hands. Family troubles, Jack."

"Well, come on in. You're here without your hat. Want to get your death of cold?" growled Mr. Canary.

The young folks did not dream at this time that nature was doing her best to make it impossible for Ida Bellethorne to reach New York by Sunday morning when the steamship *San Salvador* would leave her dock. It was, however, the general topic of conversation during the evening. When bed-time came they went gaily to bed, not even Betty doubting the feasibility of their getting to the train on the morrow.

Her uncle, however, put his head out of the door again when the others had gone chamberward and seeing the shining, icy waste of the Overlook, muttered with growing anxiety:

"Can it be done?"

CHAPTER XXIV

TWENTY MILES OF GRADE

Ida slept in the room with Betty and Bobby that night. Betty had confided to her chum, as well as to Uncle Dick, the outcome of the mystery of her locket. Because of Ida's information, Uncle Dick had assured his niece they would recover the trinket.

"If Mrs. Staples is not a dishonest woman, she shades that character pretty closely. There are people like that—people who think that a found article is their own unless absolutely claimed by the victim of the loss. A rather prejudiced brand of honesty to say the least."

The two Shadyside girls made much of Ida Bellethorne on this evening after they had fore-gathered in the bedroom. Just think! her Aunt Ida might take her to South America. Ida already had traveled by boat much farther than even Betty had journeyed by train.

"Although I am not at all sure how my aunt will meet me," the English girl said. "She was very angry with my father. She wasn't fair to him. She is impulsive and proud, and maybe she will think no better of me. But I must give her father's letter and see what comes of it."

The main difficulty was to get to New York in time to deliver the letter before the *San Salvador* sailed. When the girls awoke very early and saw a sliver of moon shining low in the sky, they bounced up with glad if muffled cries, believing that everything was all right. The storm had ceased. And when they pushed up the window a little more to stick their heads out they immediately discovered something else.

"Goodness me!" gasped Bobby. "It's one glare of ice—everything! And so-o cold! Ugh!" and she shivered, bundled as she was in a blanket robe.

First Betty and then Ida had to investigate. The latter looked very mournful.

"The horse can never travel to-day," she groaned. "You saw how he slipped about in the soft snow the other day when they had him out. He is not shod properly."

"If you only had Ida Bellethorne here!" cried Betty.

"But she is a long way off, and in the wrong direction. Why, none of us could walk on this ice!"

"How about skating?" cried Bobby eagerly.

"Mr. Canary says it is all downhill—or mostly to the railroad station," Betty said. "I would be afraid to skate downhill."

They dressed quickly and hastened to find Uncle Dick. He had long been up and had evidently canvassed the situation thoroughly. His face was very grave when he met his niece and her friends.

"This is a bad lookout for our trip," he said. "I don't really

Alice B. Emerson

see how any of you will get to school on Monday, let alone Ida's reaching New York to-morrow morning."

"Oh, Uncle Dick, don't say that!" cried Betty. "Is it positive that we cannot ride or walk?"

"Walk twenty miles downhill on ice?" he exclaimed, "Does it seem reasonable? We can neither ride nor walk; and surely we cannot swim or fly!"

"We could fly if we had an aeroplane. Oh, dear!" sighed Bobby. "Why didn't we think of that? And now the telephone wires are down."

But Betty was thoughtful. She only pinched Ida's arm and begged her to keep up her courage—perhaps something would turn up. She disappeared then and was absent from the house, cold as the morning was, until breakfast time.

The whole party had gathered then, excited and voluble. It was not only regarding Ida's need that they chattered so eagerly. In spite of the fun they were having at Mountain Camp, the thought that Shadyside and Salsette might begin classes before they could get there was, after all, rather shocking.

"Measles is one thing," said Bob. "But being out of bounds when classes really begin is another. The other fellows will learn some tricks that we don't know."

"And somebody else may be put in our room, Betty!" wailed Bobby, as her chum now appeared.

Betty was very rosy and full of something that was bound to spill over at once. As soon as she had bidden Mr. and Mrs. Canary good morning she cried to all:

"What do you think!"

"Just as little as possible," declared Tommy Tucker. "Thinking tires me dreadfully."

"Behave, Tommy!" said Louise admonishingly.

"There's a big two-horse pung here. I found it in the barn. Like Mr. Jaroth's. It has a deep box like his. And a tongue. It's like a double-runner sled, Bob—you know. The front runners are independent of the rear."

"I know what it is, Betty," said Bob, while the others stared at her. "I've seen that pung."

"Your observations are correct, Miss Betty," said Mr. Canary, smiling at the girl. "I own such a pung. But I do not own two horses to draw it. And I am sorry to say that the horse I have got cannot stand on this ice."

"Gee!" exclaimed Teddy, "if we got old Bobsky started down that hill he'd never stop till he got to the bottom. How far do you say it is to the station, Mr. Canary?"

"It is quite twenty miles down grade. Of course there are several places where the road is level—or was level before the snow fell. But once started there would not be many places where you would have to get out and push," and the gentleman laughed.

Betty's mind was fixed upon her argument. Her face still glowed and she scarcely tasted her breakfast.

"I believe we can do it," she murmured.

"What under the sun do you mean, Betty?" asked Louise.

Alice B. Emerson

"I hope it is something nice we can do," said Libbie dreamily. "I looked out the window and it is all like fairyland—isn't it, Timothy?"

"Uh-huh!" said Timothy Derby, his mouth rather full at the moment. "It is the most beautiful sight I ever saw. Will you please pass me another muffin?"

But Bob gave Betty his undivided attention. He asked:

"What do you believe we can do, Betty?"

"Make use of Mr. Canary's pung."

"Cricky! What will draw it? Where is the span of noble steeds to be found? Old Bobsky would break his neck."

"One horse. One wonderful horse, Bob!" cried Betty clapping her hands suddenly. "I am sure I'm right. Uncle Dick!"

"What do you mean, Betty?" cried Bobby, shaking her. "What horse?"

"Gravitation," announced Betty, her eyes shining. "That's his name."

"Great goodness!" gasped Bob. "I see a light. But Betty, how'd we steer it?"

"The front runners are attached to the tongue. Tie ropes to the tongue and steer it that way," Betty said, so eagerly that her words tumbled over each other. "Can't we do it, Uncle Dick? We'll all pile into the pung, with a lot of straw to keep us warm, and just slide down the hills to the railroad station. What say?"

For a while there was a good deal said by all present. Mr. and Mrs. Canary at first scouted the reasonableness of the idea. But Mr. Gordon, being an engineer and, as Bob said, "up to all such problems," considered Betty's suggestion carefully.

In the first place the need was serious. Especially for the much troubled Ida. If she could not reach the dock on New York's water-front by eleven o'clock the next morning, her aunt would doubtless sail on the *San Salvador*, and then there was no knowing when the English girl would be able to find her only living relative.

The party had ridden over the mountain road in coming to Mountain Camp, and Uncle Dick remembered the course pretty well. Although it was a continual grade, as one might say, it was an easy grade. And there were few turns in the road.

Drifted with snow as it was, and that snow crusted, the idea of coasting all the way to the railroad station did not seem so wild a thought. The road was fenced for most of the way on both sides. And over those fences the drifts rose smoothly, making almost a trough of the road.

"When you come to think of it, Jack," Uncle Dick said to Mr. Canary, "it is not very different from our toboggan chute yonder. Only it is longer."

"A good bit longer," said Mr. Canary, shaking his head.

However, it was plain that the idea interested Uncle Dick. He hastened out to look at the pung. Bob followed him, and they were gone half an hour or more. When they returned Bob was grinning broadly.

Alice B. Emerson

"Get ready for the time of your lives, girls," he whispered to Betty and Bobby. "The thing is going to work. You wait and see!"

Uncle Dick called them all into the living room and told them to pack at once and prepare for a cold ride. There was plenty of time, for the train they had to catch did not reach the station until noon.

"If our trip is successful—and it will be, I feel sure—it will not take an hour to reach the station. But we shall give ourselves plenty of time. Now off with you! I guess Mrs. Canary will be glad to see the last of us."

But their hostess denied this. The delight of having young people at the lonely camp in the hills quite counterbalanced the disturbance they made. But she bustled about somewhat anxiously, aiding the girls and the boys to make ready for departure. The Canarys, being unused to roughing it, even if they did live in the Big Woods, were much more afraid of the possibility of an accident arising out of this scheme Betty had conceived than was Uncle Dick.

A little after ten o'clock they all piled out of the bungalow with their baggage. The two men working at the camp had filled the box of the pung with straw and had drawn it out to the brow of the hill where the road began. The tongue was raised at a slant, as high as it would go, and half of it had been sawed off. Ropes were fastened from this stub of the tongue to ringbolts on either side of the pung-box.

"It will take two of us to steer," said Uncle Dick, "and we must work together. Get in here, Bob, and I'll show you how it works."

It worked easily. The girls and the baggage were piled into

the pung. The Tucker twins were each handed an iron-shod woodsman's peavey and were shown how the speed of the pung might be retarded by dragging them in the crust on either side.

"You boys are the brakes," sang out Uncle Dick, almost as excited as the young people themselves. "When we shout for 'Brakes!' it is up to you twins to do your part."

"We will, sir!" cried Tommy and Teddy in unison.

"And don't hang your arms or legs over the sides," advised Uncle Dick. "Farewell, Jack! Take care of him, Mrs. Canary. And many, many thanks for a jolly time."

The boys and girls chorused their gratitude to the owner of Mountain Camp and his wife. The men behind gave the pung just the tiniest push. The runners creaked over the ice, and the forward end pitched down the slope. They had started.

And what a ride that was! It is not likely that any of them will ever forget it. Yet, as it proved, the danger was slight. They coasted the entire down-grade to the little railroad station where Fred Jaroth was telegraph operator with scarcely more peril than as though they had been riding behind the Jaroth horses.

But they were on the *qui vive* all the time. Bobby declared her heart was in her mouth so much that she could taste it.

There were places when the speed threatened disaster. But when Uncle Dick shouted for "Brakes!" the twins broke through the crust with their peaveys and the hook broke up the thick ice and dragged back on the pung so that the latter was brought almost to a stop. The handles of the peaveys were braced against the end staffs of the pung, and to keep

Alice B. Emerson

them in position did not exceed the twins' strength.

Once Ted's peavey was dragged from his hands; but he jumped out and recovered it, and then, falling, slid flat on his back down the slippery way until he overtook the slowly moving pung again amid the delighted shouts of his chums.

Otherwise there were no casualties, and the pung flew past the Jaroth house a little before eleven to the great amazement of the whole family, who ran out to watch the coasting party.

"I don't know how Jonathan Canary will recover his pung," said Mr. Gordon when they alighted on the level ground. "But I will leave it in Jaroth's care, and when the winter breaks up, or before, it can be taken back to Mountain Camp.

"Now how do you feel, young folks? All right? No bones broken?"

"It was delightful," they cried. But Ida added something to this. "I feel rather—rather dazed, Mr. Gordon," she said. "But I am very thankful. And I know whom I have most to thank."

"Who is that; my dear?" asked Uncle Dick smiling.

"Betty."

CHAPTER XXV

ON THE DECK OF THE SAN SALVADOR

Mr. Richard Gordon sent several telegrams before the train arrived, and they were all of importance. One recovered Betty's locket, for, informed of the circumstances by this telegram, the lawyer in Washington sent his clerk to Mrs. Staples and showed her in a very few words that she was coasting very close to the law by keeping the little platinum and diamond locket.

"So," said Betty to Bobby, "if the lawyer gets it—and Uncle Dick says he will—I can wear the locket to parties at the school."

"If Mrs. Eustice allows it," said her chum grimly. "You know, she's down on jewelry. Remember how she got after Ada Nansen and Ruth Gladys Royal for wearing so much junk?"

"My goodness!" giggled Betty, "what would she say to you if she heard you use such an expression? Anyway, I am going to show her Uncle Dick's present and ask her. I know the beautiful diamond earrings Doctor and Mrs. Guerin sent me can't be worn till I grow up a bit. But my locket is just right."

Alice B. Emerson

It was a noisy crowd that boarded the train; and it continued to be a noisy crowd to the junction where it broke up. All the young folks would have been glad to go with Uncle Dick and Ida Bellethorne to New York; but he sent all but Betty and Bob on to school. They would reach the Shadyside station soon after daybreak the next morning, and Mr. Gordon had telegraphed ahead for the school authorities to be on the look-out for them.

Betty and Bob, with Uncle Dick and the English girl, left the train at the junction and boarded another for New York City in some confidence of reaching their destination in good season.

The train, however, was late. It seemed merely to creep along for miles and miles. Luckily they had secured berths, and while they slept the delayed train did most of its creeping.

But in the morning they were dismayed to find that they were already two hours late and that it would be impossible for the train to pick up those two hours before reaching the Grand Central Terminal in New York City.

"Now, hold your horses, young people!" advised Mr. Gordon. "We are not beaten yet. The *San Salvador* does not leave her dock until eleven at the earliest. It may be several hours later. I have wired to Miss Bellethorne aboard the ship and in care of the Toscanelli Opera Company as well. I do not know the hotel at which Miss Bellethorne has been staying."

"But, Uncle Dick!" cried Betty, who seemed to have thought of every chance that might arise, "suppose Ida's aunt wants to take her along to Brazil? Her passport—"

"Can be vised at the British consulate on Whitehall Street in a very few minutes. I have examined Ida's passport, and there is no reason why there should be any trouble over it at all. She is a minor, you see, and if her aunt wishes to assume responsibility for her no effort will be made to keep her in the country, that is sure."

"Then it all depends upon Ida's aunt," sighed Betty.

"And our reaching the dock in time," amended Uncle Dick. "I would not wish to interfere with Miss Bellethorne's business engagement in Rio Janeiro; but I am anxious for her to authorize me, on behalf of her niece, to get legal matters in train for the recovery of that beautiful mare. I believe that she belongs—every hair and hoof of her—to our young friend here. There has been some trickery in the case."

"Oh, Uncle Dick!" shrieked Betty.

"When I went to see that poor little cripple Hunchie Slattery he told me that the very papers that were given to Mr. Bolter with the horse must prove Ida's ownership at one time of the mare. There was some kind of a quit-claim deed signed by her name, and that signature must be a forgery.

"The horse could never have been sold in England, for the Bellethorne stable was too well known there. The men who grabbed the string of horses left when Ida's father died are well-to-do, and Mr. Bolter will be able to get his money back, even if he has already paid the full price agreed upon for Ida Bellethorne.

"I am convinced," concluded Uncle Dick, "that the girl has something coming to her. And it may even pay Miss Bellethorne to remain in the United States instead of going to Rio Janeiro until the matter of the black mare's ownership is

Alice B. Emerson

settled beyond any doubt."

When the train finally reached New York, Uncle Dick did not even delay to try to reach the dock by telephone. He bundled his party into a taxicab and they were transported to the dock where the *San Salvador* lay.

A steward seemed to be on the look-out for the party, and addressed Uncle Dick the moment he alighted from the cab.

"Mr. Gordon, sir? Yes, sir. Madam Bellethorne has received your wire and is waiting for you. I have arranged for you all to be passed through the inspection line. The steamship, sir, is delayed and will not sail until next tide."

"And that is a mighty good thing for us," declared Mr. Gordon to his charges.

His business card helped get them past the inspectors. It is not easy to board a ship nowadays to bid good-bye to a sailing friend. But in ten minutes or so they stood before the great singer.

She was a tall and handsome woman. Betty at first glance saw that Ida, the niece, would very likely grow into a very close resemblance to Madam Bellethorne.

The woman looked swiftly from Betty to Ida and made no mistake in her identification of her brother's daughter. Ida was crying just a little, but when she realized how close and kindly was her aunt's embrace she shook the drops out of her eyes and smiled.

"Father wanted I should find you, Aunt Ida," she said. "He wrote a letter to you and I have it. I think it was the principal thing he thought of during his last illness—his misunderstanding with you."

"My fault as much as his," Madam Bellethorne said sadly. "We were both proud and high-tempered. But no more of this now. Something in this gentleman's long telegram to me—"

She bowed to Mr. Gordon. He quickly stated the matter of the black mare's ownership to the singer.

"If you will come to the British consulate where Ida's passport must be vised, and sign there a paper empowering me to act in your behalf, you assuming the guardianship of Ida, I can start lawyers on the trail of this swindle."

Miss Bellethorne was a woman of prompt decision and of a business mind, and immediately agreed. She likewise saw that her niece had made powerful friends during the weeks she had been in America and she was content to allow Mr. Gordon to do the girl this kindness.

It was a busy time; but the delay in the sailing of the *San Salvador* made it possible for everything necessary to be accomplished. Uncle Dick and Betty and Bob accompanied the Bellethornes aboard the ship again and had luncheon with them. Ida cried when she parted with Betty; but it would be only for the winter. When the opera company returned to New York it was already planned that the younger Ida Bellethorne should join the friends of her own age she had so recently made at Shadyside School.

It was an astonishing sight for Betty and Bob to see the great ship worried out of her dock by the fussy little tugs. It was growing dark by that time and the great steamship was brilliantly lighted. They watched until she was in midstream and was headed down the harbor under her own steam.

Alice B. Emerson

"There! It's over!" sighed Betty. "I feel as if a great load had been lifted from my mind. Dear me, Bob! do you suppose we can ever again have so much excitement crowded into a few hours?"

As Betty was no seeress and could not see into the future she of course did not dream that in a very few weeks, and in very different surroundings, she would experience adventures quite as interesting as any which had already come into her life. These will be published in the next volume of this series, entitled: "Betty Gordon at Ocean Park; or, Gay Doings on the Boardwalk."

Bob shook his head at Betty's last observation. "Does seem as though we manage to get hooked up to lots of strange folks and strange happenings. Certain metals attract lightning, Betty, and I think you attract adventures. What do you say, Uncle Dick?"

Mr. Gordon only laughed. "I say that you young folks had better have supper and a long night's rest. I shall not let you go on to school until to-morrow. For once you will be a day late; but I will chance explaining the circumstances to your instructors."

They got into the taxicab again and bowled away up town. The lights came up like rows of fireflies in the cross streets. When they struck into the foot of Fifth Avenue at the Washington Arch the globes on that thoroughfare were all alight. It was late enough for the traffic to have thinned out and their driver could travel at good speed save when the red lights flashed up on the traffic towers.

"Isn't this wonderful?" said Betty. "Libbie is always enthusing about pretty views and fairylike landscapes. What would she and Timothy say to this?"

"Something silly, I bet," grumbled Bob. "Cricky! but I'm hungry," proving by this speech that he had a soul at this moment very little above mundane things.

Uncle Dick chuckled in his corner of the car, and made no comment. And Betty said nothing further just then. The brilliant lights of the avenue were shining full in her face, but her thoughts were far away, with Ida Bellethorne on that ocean-going steamer bound for South America. What a wonderful winter of adventures it had been!

"And the best of it is, it all came out right in the end," murmured the girl softly to herself.

Alice B. Emerson

Choose from Thousands of 1stWorldLibrary Classics By

A. M. Barnard
Ada Leverson
Adolphus William Ward
Aesop
Agatha Christie
Alexander Aaronsohn
Alexander Kielland
Alexandre Dumas
Alfred Gatty
Alfred Ollivant
Alice Duer Miller
Alice Turner Curtis
Alice Dunbar
Allen Chapman
Alleyne Ireland
Ambrose Bierce
Amelia E. Barr
Amory H. Bradford
Andrew Lang
Andrew McFarland Davis
Andy Adams
Angela Brazil
Anna Alice Chapin
Anna Sewell
Annie Besant
Annie Hamilton Donnell
Annie Payson Call
Annie Roe Carr
Annonaymous
Anton Chekhov
Archibald Lee Fletcher
Arnold Bennett
Arthur C. Benson
Arthur Conan Doyle
Arthur M. Winfield
Arthur Ransome
Arthur Schnitzler
Arthur Train
Atticus
B.H. Baden-Powell
B. M. Bower
B. C. Chatterjee
Baroness Emmuska Orczy
Baroness Orczy
Basil King
Bayard Taylor
Ben Macomber
Bertha Muzzy Bower
Bjornstjerne Bjornson

Booth Tarkington
Boyd Cable
Bram Stoker
C. Collodi
C. E. Orr
C. M. Ingleby
Carolyn Wells
Catherine Parr Traill
Charles A. Eastman
Charles Amory Beach
Charles Dickens
Charles Dudley Warner
Charles Farrar Browne
Charles Ives
Charles Kingsley
Charles Klein
Charles Hanson Towne
Charles Lathrop Pack
Charles Romyn Dake
Charles Whibley
Charles Willing Beale
Charlotte M. Braeme
Charlotte M. Yonge
Charlotte Perkins Stetson
Clair W. Hayes
Clarence Day Jr.
Clarence E. Mulford
Clemence Housman
Confucius
Coningsby Dawson
Cornelis DeWitt Wilcox
Cyril Burleigh
D. H. Lawrence
Daniel Defoe
David Garnett
Dinah Craik
Don Carlos Janes
Donald Keyhoe
Dorothy Kilner
Dougan Clark
Douglas Fairbanks
E. Nesbit
E. P. Roe
E. Phillips Oppenheim
E. S. Brooks
Earl Barnes
Edgar Rice Burroughs
Edith Van Dyne
Edith Wharton

Edward Everett Hale
Edward J. O'Biren
Edward S. Ellis
Edwin L. Arnold
Eleanor Atkins
Eleanor Hallowell Abbott
Eliot Gregory
Elizabeth Gaskell
Elizabeth McCracken
Elizabeth Von Arnim
Ellem Key
Emerson Hough
Emilie F. Carlen
Emily Bronte
Emily Dickinson
Enid Bagnold
Enilor Macartney Lane
Erasmus W. Jones
Ernie Howard Pie
Ethel May Dell
Ethel Turner
Ethel Watts Mumford
Eugene Sue
Eugenie Foa
Eugene Wood
Eustace Hale Ball
Evelyn Everett-green
Everard Cotes
F. H. Cheley
F. J. Cross
F. Marion Crawford
Fannie E. Newberry
Federick Austin Ogg
Ferdinand Ossendowski
Fergus Hume
Florence A. Kilpatrick
Fremont B. Deering
Francis Bacon
Francis Darwin
Frances Hodgson Burnett
Frances Parkinson Keyes
Frank Gee Patchin
Frank Harris
Frank Jewett Mather
Frank L. Packard
Frank V. Webster
Frederic Stewart Isham
Frederick Trevor Hill
Frederick Winslow Taylor

Friedrich Kerst
Friedrich Nietzsche
Fyodor Dostoyevsky
G.A. Henty
G.K. Chesterton
Gabrielle E. Jackson
Garrett P. Serviss
Gaston Leroux
George A. Warren
George Ade
Geroge Bernard Shaw
George Cary Eggleston
George Durston
George Ebers
George Eliot
George Gissing
George MacDonald
George Meredith
George Orwell
George Sylvester Viereck
George Tucker
George W. Cable
George Wharton James
Gertrude Atherton
Gordon Casserly
Grace E. King
Grace Gallatin
Grace Greenwood
Grant Allen
Guillermo A. Sherwell
Gulielma Zollinger
Gustav Flaubert
H. A. Cody
H. B. Irving
H.C. Bailey
H. G. Wells
H. H. Munro
H. Irving Hancock
H. R. Naylor
H. Rider Haggard
H. W. C. Davis
Haldeman Julius
Hall Caine
Hamilton Wright Mabie
Hans Christian Andersen
Harold Avery
Harold McGrath
Harriet Beecher Stowe
Harry Castlemon
Harry Coghill
Harry Houidini

Hayden Carruth
Helent Hunt Jackson
Helen Nicolay
Hendrik Conscience
Hendy David Thoreau
Henri Barbusse
Henrik Ibsen
Henry Adams
Henry Ford
Henry Frost
Henry James
Henry Jones Ford
Henry Seton Merriman
Henry W Longfellow
Herbert A. Giles
Herbert Carter
Herbert N. Casson
Herman Hesse
Hildegard G. Frey
Homer
Honore De Balzac
Horace B. Day
Horace Walpole
Horatio Alger Jr.
Howard Pyle
Howard R. Garis
Hugh Lofting
Hugh Walpole
Humphry Ward
Ian Maclaren
Inez Haynes Gillmore
Irving Bacheller
Isabel Cecilia Williams
Isabel Hornibrook
Israel Abrahams
Ivan Turgenev
J.G.Austin
J. Henri Fabre
J. M. Barrie
J. M. Walsh
J. Macdonald Oxley
J. R. Miller
J. S. Fletcher
J. S. Knowles
J. Storer Clouston
J. W. Duffield
Jack London
Jacob Abbott
James Allen
James Andrews
James Baldwin

James Branch Cabell
James DeMille
James Joyce
James Lane Allen
James Lane Allen
James Oliver Curwood
James Oppenheim
James Otis
James R. Driscoll
Jane Abbott
Jane Austen
Jane L. Stewart
Janet Aldridge
Jens Peter Jacobsen
Jerome K. Jerome
Jessie Graham Flower
John Buchan
John Burroughs
John Cournos
John F. Kennedy
John Gay
John Glasworthy
John Habberton
John Joy Bell
John Kendrick Bangs
John Milton
John Philip Sousa
John Taintor Foote
Jonas Lauritz Idemil Lie
Jonathan Swift
Joseph A. Altsheler
Joseph Carey
Joseph Conrad
Joseph E. Badger Jr
Joseph Hergesheimer
Joseph Jacobs
Jules Vernes
Julian Hawthrone
Julie A Lippmann
Justin Huntly McCarthy
Kakuzo Okakura
Karle Wilson Baker
Kate Chopin
Kenneth Grahame
Kenneth McGaffey
Kate Langley Bosher
Kate Langley Bosher
Katherine Cecil Thurston
Katherine Stokes
L. A. Abbot
L. T. Meade

L. Frank Baum
Latta Griswold
Laura Dent Crane
Laura Lee Hope
Laurence Housman
Lawrence Beasley
Leo Tolstoy
Leonid Andreyev
Lewis Carroll
Lewis Sperry Chafer
Lilian Bell
Lloyd Osbourne
Louis Hughes
Louis Joseph Vance
Louis Tracy
Louisa May Alcott
Lucy Fitch Perkins
Lucy Maud Montgomery
Luther Benson
Lydia Miller Middleton
Lyndon Orr
M. Corvus
M. H. Adams
Margaret E. Sangster
Margret Howth
Margaret Vandercook
Margaret W. Hungerford
Margret Penrose
Maria Edgeworth
Maria Thompson Daviess
Mariano Azuela
Marion Polk Angellotti
Mark Overton
Mark Twain
Mary Austin
Mary Catherine Crowley
Mary Cole
Mary Hastings Bradley
Mary Roberts Rinehart
Mary Rowlandson
M. Wollstonecraft Shelley
Maud Lindsay
Max Beerbohm
Myra Kelly
Nathaniel Hawthrone
Nicolo Machiavelli
O. F. Walton
Oscar Wilde

Owen Johnson
P.G. Wodehouse
Paul and Mabel Thorne
Paul G. Tomlinson
Paul Severing
Percy Brebner
Percy Keese Fitzhugh
Peter B. Kyne
Plato
Quincy Allen
R. Derby Holmes
R. L. Stevenson
R. S. Ball
Rabindranath Tagore
Rahul Alvares
Ralph Bonehill
Ralph Henry Barbour
Ralph Victor
Ralph Waldo Emmerson
Rene Descartes
Ray Cummings
Rex Beach
Rex E. Beach
Richard Harding Davis
Richard Jefferies
Richard Le Gallienne
Robert Barr
Robert Frost
Robert Gordon Anderson
Robert L. Drake
Robert Lansing
Robert Lynd
Robert Michael Ballantyne
Robert W. Chambers
Rosa Nouchette Carey
Rudyard Kipling
Saint Augustine
Samuel B. Allison
Samuel Hopkins Adams
Sarah Bernhardt
Sarah C. Hallowell
Selma Lagerlof
Sherwood Anderson
Sigmund Freud
Standish O'Grady
Stanley Weyman
Stella Benson
Stella M. Francis

Stephen Crane
Stewart Edward White
Stijn Streuvels
Swami Abhedananda
Swami Parmananda
T. S. Ackland
T. S. Arthur
The Princess Der Ling
Thomas A. Janvier
Thomas A Kempis
Thomas Anderton
Thomas Bailey Aldrich
Thomas Bulfinch
Thomas De Quincey
Thomas Dixon
Thomas H. Huxley
Thomas Hardy
Thomas More
Thornton W. Burgess
U. S. Grant
Upton Sinclair
Valentine Williams
Various Authors
Vaughan Kester
Victor Appleton
Victor G. Durham
Victoria Cross
Virginia Woolf
Wadsworth Camp
Walter Camp
Walter Scott
Washington Irving
Wilbur Lawton
Wilkie Collins
Willa Cather
Willard F. Baker
William Dean Howells
William le Queux
W. Makepeace Thackeray
William W. Walter
William Shakespeare
Winston Churchill
Yei Theodora Ozaki
Yogi Ramacharaka
Young E. Allison
Zane Grey